OPERATION ZITADELLE 1943

OPERATION ZITADELLE 1943
THE GREATEST TANK BATTLE

MARK HEALY

The History Press

Front cover illustration: T-34s launch an attack against oncoming Germans.

First published 2012 as *Kursk 1943: Battle Story* by Spellmount
This paperback edition first published 2023

The History Press
97 St George's Place, Cheltenham,
Gloucestershire, GL50 3QB
www.thehistorypress.co.uk

British Library Cataloguing in Publication Data.
A catalogue record for this book is available from the British Library.

ISBN 978 1 80399 343 0

Typesetting and origination by The History Press
Printed and bound in Great Britain by TJ Books Limited, Padstow, Cornwall

MIX
Paper from
responsible sources
FSC
www.fsc.org   FSC® C013056

Trees for LYfe

CONTENTS

Introduction	7
Timeline	14
Historical Background	20
Conceiving the Plans: Rastenburg and the Kremlin	20
The Battlefield	28
The Armies	31
The Commanders	31
The Soldiers	40
The Kit	43
The Days Before Battle	56
The German Plan	56
The Preparatory Period, April–5 July	58
The Citadel	60
The German Tactics	69
The German Offensive	75
5 July Zitadelle Begins	75
6–11 July 4th Panzer Army	94
6–12 July Ninth Army	114
12–17 July Prokhorovka	125
The Legacy	138
The Cost	141

Orders of Battle 146
Visiting the Battlefield 152
Further Reading 153
Index 155

INTRODUCTION

On 5 July 1943, the last great German offensive on the Eastern Front began. It was directed at the destruction of the Kursk salient in the eastern Ukraine and constituted a last, supreme effort by the Germans to stabilise the Eastern Front in the face of ever burgeoning Soviet military power. It failed. Thereafter, with the strategic initiative having been irrevocably lost, the Germans began a fighting retreat that did not end until two years later when the Red Army stormed Berlin and Adolf Hitler committed suicide in his bunker.

This was not the outcome envisaged by the German leader when he penned War Directive Number 21, in December 1940. In that document he assumed, as did the senior commanders of the Wehrmacht, that a 'rapid campaign' against the Soviet Union would be little different in outcome and just a little longer in duration than that which had brought France, Belgium and Holland to defeat in six weeks half a year earlier. Indeed, Operation *Barbarossa* – the code name adopted for the invasion of Russia in June 1941 – was based upon a number of fatally erroneous assumptions about Nazi Germany's eastern ally. Hitler and the Wehrmacht's low opinion of the Soviet state and its armed forces, his hatred of its communist ideology and above all, his racist perception of its Slavic people as *untermenschen* – sub humans – all served to feed his conviction that the USSR was 'a colossus with feet of clay' such that we 'have only to kick in the front door and the whole rotten structure will come tumbling down.'

In the months between the invasion of Russia on 22 June 1941 and March 1942, the Wehrmacht had conquered large areas of the western USSR and captured and killed over five million Red Army soldiers. But it had also suffered its first strategic reverse, which served to puncture the reputation for invincibility that the Wehrmacht had acquired since September 1939. The Red Army counter offensive begun on 5 December, which had hurled the German forces back from the approaches to Moscow, had then grown into an effort that embraced the full extent of the Eastern Front by the end of January 1942. When, at the end of March, it petered out owing to the thaw and the exhaustion of the combatants, the Soviet Union was far from being finished, and Nazi Germany a very long way from realising victory over erstwhile ally.

The massive reduction of German military strength incurred in the first ten months of the Eastern Campaign brought about a contraction of Germany's strategic aspiration for the summer of 1942. Hitler would have no truck with a defensive posture and with the onset of the wider war, it was deemed imperative that the USSR be defeated in 1942. It was to service Germany's wider war aims and also secure Russia's collapse that Hitler eschewed any renewed attempt to take Moscow. Rather, the German offensive effort was to be directed towards the realisation of primarily economic objectives. As early as January, Hitler had indicated that the priority objective for the coming summer campaign must be the capture and exploitation of the oilfields of the Caucasus, without which, he told one audience: 'I must end this war.' It was for this reason that a secondary objective of Case Blue – as the 1942 offensive had been named – was to bring the city of Stalingrad under fire so as to interdict the oil supplies taken by barge from Baku northward along the river Volga.

It was against this backdrop that Case Blue opened on 28 June. Once more the panzer divisions gobbled up space and advanced headlong across the steppe in the face of what appeared to be a totally demoralised Red Army. But this was more apparent than

8

real as by October the German advance had ground to a halt along the foothills of the Caucasus and Sixth Army was embroiled in a ferocious battle of attrition amidst the ruins of the city of Stalingrad. One month later and the chickens came home to roost. On 22 November, the Red Army launched a major offensive and encircled the city. Hitler's response was to order Sixth Army to remain in place, 'on the Volga'.

Hitler now appointed Field Marshal Erich von Manstein to oversee Army Group Don – a new and hastily assembled command – and tasked him with relieving Stalingrad. The day before this formation's subsequently abortive attack began on 12 December, German forces began their withdrawal from the Caucasus. By the end of the month, the German line along the Don, to the north of Stalingrad, was disintegrating as Axis armies succumbed to the widening Soviet offensive. On 10 January 1943, the Red Army launched the final reduction of the Stalingrad pocket. Hitler ordered 1st Panzer Army out of the Caucasus on 24 January to reinforce Manstein's weakened forces protecting the Donetz industrial region. Along the Don front, a number of Soviet Fronts had vanquished the remnants of Axis forces, such that by 2 February, the Voronezh Front had crossed the Donets and was threatening Kharkov. Strength returns indicated that as of 23 January, the *Ostheer* could only field 495 operational tanks.

It was against this backdrop that on 6 February, just three days after the surrender of Stalingrad was announced in Germany, Manstein met with Hitler at his headquarters at Rastenburg in East Prussia. Among the items discussed was the strategy to be adopted by the *Heer* for the summer. Of the two operational options he proffered to Hitler, Manstein was in favour of the 'backhand'. This presumed that the Red Army would launch a massive offensive in southern Russia in the summer that should be allowed to mature, with German forces falling back so as to permit the Soviets to overextend themselves. At the right moment, a massive armoured counter attack would be launched, catching the Red Army on 'the backhand'. This would then drive southward and pin them against

Operation Zitadelle 1943

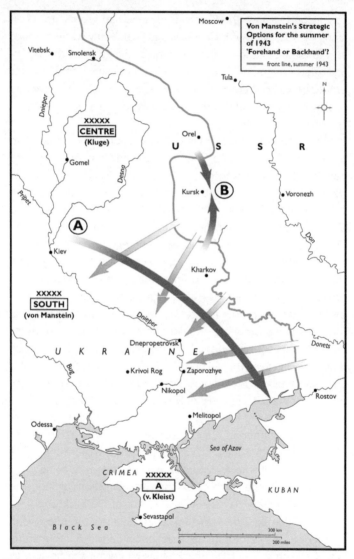

Manstein's proposals to Hitler for 1943. (A) The backhand – await the Russian summer offensive then defeat it. (B) The forehand – an early offensive to destroy the Kursk salient drawing the Red Army's teeth for the rest of the summer by the infliction of catastrophic losses.

the Sea of Azov. The outcome of such a victory would, Manstein believed, generate the conditions whereby the Soviets would be forcibly encouraged into some sort of political arrangement to end the war. Manstein never revealed this political dimension of his proposal, as he knew Hitler would have baulked immediately as the German leader would have no truck with such thinking.

Manstein's alternative option, which he called the 'forehand', turned on the Germans seizing the offensive initiative to inflict an early and heavy defeat on the Red Army as soon as the weather and ground were dry enough to allow the panzers to operate. Not surprisingly, with the front in the south seemingly on the verge of disintegration, this discussion was not taken further. Nonetheless, a seed had been planted in Hitler's mind with the 'forehand' proposal and this would bear fruit within months with the issue of plans for a limited offensive in the early summer.

By 9 February, Soviet forces were approaching Kharkov from the north and south. Two days later, the SS Panzer Corps had been pushed back into the city. On the 11th, German forces were ordered by Hitler to hold the city 'at all costs', whilst in the gap that had opened up in the German front between Kharkov and Orel, General Vatutin, the commander of the Voronezh Front, was prompted by Stalin into ordering his 6th Army to advance and take Zaporozhye. As of 13 January, this vital city crossing point over the Dnieper had become the site of Manstein's headquarters in his new role as commander of Army Group South.

Matters in Kharkov now came to a head. On the 15th, with the total encirclement of the city in prospect and the inevitable loss of his units in consequence, *Obergruppenführer* Hausser unilaterally ordered his force to begin withdrawal from the city, only to receive yet another 'hold' order. On this occasion Hausser ignored his immediate superior as well as Hitler. The withdrawal proceeded. In an act of unprecedented disobedience, the head of the SS Panzer Corps had chosen to save his force notwithstanding his allegiance to Hitler. By his action, Hausser saved his force to fight another day, and indeed, what was to follow – the German counter offensive that

Hitler visited von Manstein for a second time in at Zaporozhye on 10 March 1943. The subject of the summer campaign was discussed.

within the month saw the re-capture of Kharkov – would not have been possible had he not done so.

Hitler now flew out to see Manstein at his headquarters. After days of hard debate, the Führer conceded to the Field Marshal's demand that in the face of the dire situation facing Army Group South, he be given ' a free hand' to conduct operations as he saw fit.

Manstein now began a concentration and re-deployment of his forces, unleashing his mobile formations on 18 February against a surprised enemy who had totally misinterpreted German intentions. Lulled by wishful thinking, Stavka had attributed the German withdrawals as signs of their imminent complete collapse and evidence of a full-scale retreat westward across the Dnieper. In a classic demonstration of mobile warfare, 1st Panzer Army and Hoth's 4th Panzer Army, the latter with the three divisions of the SS Panzer Corps operating as its cutting edge, excised enemy mobile spearheads, forcing the remnants of the Soviet South-Western Front and then the Voronezh Front into a hasty retreat on the city of Kharkov and the line of the river Donets. Though it took until 14 March for SS troops from the 1st and 2nd divisions to clear all

Panzers of the I SS Panzer Grenadier Division Leibstandarte Adolf Hitler *move into Kharkov after its recapture, March 1943.*

Soviet opposition from inside Kharkov. Three days later 48th Panzer Corps and the SS Panzer Corps began their drive northward from Kharkov and advanced on the city of Belgorod.

TIMELINE

1943

2 February	Final surrender of all German forces in Stalingrad.
8 February	Soviet forces recapture Kursk
18 February–18 March	German counter-offensive recaptures much territory lost to Red Army. Kharkov retaken with heavy German losses. Manstein closes down all counter-offensive operations.
13 March	Field Marshal von Manstein receives copy of Operational Order No: 5 identifying Kursk Salient as focus of early limited German offensive by forces of Army Groups Centre and South.
25 March	Ninth Army performs completes abandonment of Rzhev Salient. It is earmarked as key offensive formation for Army Group Centre.
8–12 April	Deputy Supreme Commander Marshal Zhukov recommends to Stalin that Red Army embrace a strategic defence in the Kursk salient to defeat German offensive. Stalin concurs on 12 with adoption of a two stage defensive/counter offensive strategy. Orders construction of massive defensive fortifications in and to rear of the salient.

Timeline

15 April	Operational Order No: 6 supersedes earlier directive naming destruction of the Kursk salient by code name Operation *Zitadelle*, to begin 3 May.
5/6 May	Intelligence repudiates German assumptions about Russian intentions in the salient. Red Army now drawn up for a massive defensive. Hitler decides to persist with operation but orders first of many delays to permit addition of far larger numbers of tanks to the operation. Within days all Axis forces in North Africa surrender to western Allies.
1 July	Hitler tells his generals that as all now seems quiet in the Mediterranean, he has decided to launch *Zitadelle* on 5 July.

1943

Operation Zitadelle

1943

5–6 July **Ninth Army/Central Front**

Following the onset of the German offensive, General Rokossovsky attempts to discern the primary axis of the enemy assault. By days end this is seen to be directed to the west of the Orel/Kursk railway line. However, Model did not see fit to use his panzer divisions *en masse* from the outset but choose to feed them in over a number of days. Initial assaults by infantry supported by Tigers, Ferdinands and Assault Guns fails to achieve a rapid breakthrough.

On 6 July, Rokossovsky launches his 2nd Tank Army at the main German thrust line. Subsidiary German thrusts on either flank are held by the Soviets.

The Germans find themselves enmeshed amid minefields, massive fortifications and strong-points and make little headway.

1943

Rokossovsky begins to draw off units from formations on either side of the German flanks to bolster his defences.

5–7 July   **4th Panzer Army and Army Detachment Kempf**
Unlike Model, Hoth unleashes all of his armoured and formations at the very outset. On the left, 48th Panzer Korps makes slow headway through the Soviet defences over the first two days. On the right, II SS Panzer Korps has greater success, managing to breach the Soviet first line of defence within hours of the opening of the offensive. Although anticipating a rapid advance with Prokhorovka the Korps objective,by the end of day 2 the advance is slowing because of the immense minefields and defences.

Unnerved by the unexpected German progress through their defences, Stalin orders that the 6th Guards Tank Army, initially earmarked for counter offensive operations, be committed to prevent a German breakthrough across the river Psel. 6 GD TA begin its long journey to the Kursk battlefield where it is expected to arrive within five days to prevent a breakthrough by the Germans.

However, the inability of III Pz Kps to fully cross the Donets on Day 1 and its failure to break out of the massive Soviet defensive system by the end of Day 2, means that it is unable to fulfil its task of flank defence for the SS Pz Kps. This poses a major threat to the German timetable in the south.

7–10 July   **Ninth Army /Central Front**
Model continues to feed in his panzer divisions on a daily basis to secure a breakthrough. By the 10 July, his main thrust has advanced as far as lower slopes of the Olkhovatka heights but it is clear his offensive is running out of steam.

1943

Rokossovsky has continually drawn on other formations of his Central Front not involved in coping with the German offensive and added more and more artillery, katyusha and infantry units to continually augment his defensive field.

The German units, even though supported by extra *Luftwaffe* units sent north from the south of the salient, cannot achieve the breakthrough and dash themselves against the Soviet defences.

By day's end on the 10 July Model realises that he does not have the strength to effect the breakthrough and orders his units to engage 'in a rolling battle of attrition'. Stalin and Zhukov have already agreed on the launch date for Operation Kutuzov – the first counter offensive to be launched once they had sensed that the German offensive tide in the north was ebbing – and directed into the rear of Ninth Army to begin on the 13 July.

Zitadelle has already failed in the north.

On 10 July the Allies invade Sicily.

8–17 July   48th Pz Kps continues its advance on the Psel crossings, but its main offensive asset – the *Grossdeutschland* Pz Gren Div – now begins to find itself side-tracked into having to shore up other German formations protecting its western flank by Soviet forces that are continually attacking it. By the 10 July, this ongoing problem will see it continually involved in this fashion through to the close down of *Zitadelle*.

The Russian employ the same tactics on the SS Pz Kps eastern flank which is still devoid of its designated protection from III Pz Kps which is still immured amid the Soviet defensive system.

Operation Zitadelle 1943

1943

Nonetheless, by 9 July the SS Pz Kps is approaching the river Psel when late on that evening it begins to regroup and change its axis of advance. On the following day the Kps strikes out toward Prokhorovka.

By this date, 6th Guards TA is within striking distance of Prokhorovka and the first of its units arrive there on the following day. Also due to arrive is 5th Guards Army. German hope of a rapid advance and capture of Prokhorovka is thwarted.

On the 12 July, *Totenkopf* is engaged on the northern bank of the Psel, the *Leibstandarte Adolf Hitler* division is in the centre between the river and the Kursk/Orel railway line and *Das Reich* is operating to its south. Having regrouped his armoured units overnight, the Soviet commander of 5th Guards TA launches his forces at the Germans early on the 12 July. What has become known since as the 'Tank Battle at Prokhorovka' carries on throughout the day. Although Soviet tank losses are extremely heavy, they prevent the Germans taking Prokhorovka.

While III Pz Kps finally achieves its breakthrough to the south, it is not on hand to assist the SS Panzer Corps counter 5th GTA as the original planning had envisaged.

13–17 July Hitler tells von Manstein and von Kluge that he is terminating *Zitadelle* forthwith. The latter is pleased because he is having to deal with beginnings of a massive Soviet counter offensive against the Orel salient and is already drawing on units from Ninth Army in the salient to contest it. Manstein manages to argue for five days grace from Hitler to enable his forces to continue the destruction of Soviet armour around Prokhorovka. However, on 17 July *Zitadelle* is terminated as an offensive operation.

Timeline

1943

3 August   The Red Army launches the second of its
planned counteroffensives following on from its
defeat of the German attack on the Kursk salient.
Its launch marks the irrefutable and irrevocable
final transfer of the strategic initiative on the
Eastern Front to the Red Army.

HISTORICAL BACKGROUND

Conceiving the Plans: Rastenburg and the Kremlin

When, on 23 March 1943, von Manstein called a halt to all counter-offensive operations by Army Group South, the line reached by the German forces following the capture of Belgorod on 18 February corresponded to what would become the southern face of the Kursk salient. By that date however, Manstein knew that the destruction of the Kursk salient already figured as the primary focus of the 'limited offensive' that Hitler wished to launch as soon as the ground had dried out enough for mobile warfare. Contained in Operational Order No 5 it was given the code name *Unternehmann Zitadelle* – Operation *Citadel* – and had been received by Manstein ten days before. Hitler had thus embraced Manstein's 'forehand' proposal for an early offensive as it proffered him the opportunity of addressing pressing political, economic and military issues that were crowding his strategic horizon. An early launch of the operation and rapidity in its execution lay at the very heart of the operation. Indeed, in this Operational Order and subsequent iteration, this was deemed by Rastenburg to be its absolute *sine qua non*.

In Hitler's mind it was essential that an early and decisive defeat be inflicted on the Red Army that would serve to draw its 'offensive teeth' for the rest of the summer. The destruction of the Kursk salient would achieve this by nullifying the massing forces of two Soviet fronts that were deploying within it. He deemed such a victory to be essential to convince his wavering allies, such as the Finns, that the war in the East could still be won.

Furthermore, the immense booty and manpower that would accrue from victory would go far to helping the German war economy. Indeed, a short time before Hitler has signed a secret directive for the 'Securing of Prisoners of War, Labour Forces and Booty' that stated that a prime requirement of any offensive operation in Russia must be to secure such resources. OKW estimated that 60 Soviet divisions and between five and six armoured corps were deployed within the salient, so the booty would be extensive. The anticipated trawl of prisoners would yield between 600–700,000 men. It was intended that all would be shipped back to Germany for service as slave labour in the armaments factories and would help alleviate the shortage in manpower in German industry.

Additionally, and perhaps of overriding importance, was the deteriorating situation in the Mediterranean theatre. Following Operation *Torch* – the Anglo-American landings in North Africa the previous November – the Germans had sent substantial reinforcements into Tunisia. With the Italians already having made negative noises about the future conduct of the war, plans were being laid at Rastenburg that would address allied landings in southern Europe and which included steps to be taken should Italy try and leave the conflict. In the absence of a strategic mobile reserve in Germany to address such a contingency, Hitler would perforce have to remove such resources from the Eastern Front. Given the German leader's attachment to Mussolini and the strategic need to keep Allied forces as far away from the homeland as possible, his preference would be to pull out his 'politically reliable' troops in the form of the SS Panzer Corps for rapid deployment to Italy. As these forces were already earmarked to play a central role in *Zitadelle*, then the overwhelming requirement to launch an early offensive seemed to Hitler to be self-evident.

Operation Zitadelle 1943

That German offensive success was assured, if launched soon enough, turned on a further crucial assumption. Manstein and Hitler believed that Soviet forces in the salient would be caught by them in the process of assembling their massive forces for an offensive of their own. Hitting the Red Army at this time would find them in the process of assembling their assets and thus at their most vulnerable to the armoured assault that was the cutting edge of the German offensive design. The imperatives of time and the need to catch the Soviets forces at the right moment saw Operational Order No 5 setting the launch for the German offensive for mid-April. This was a date that, given the bad weather still obtaining in Russia at that time – with the river Donets still in full flow from the snowmelt, the ground still extremely muddy and sodden and the still exhausted nature of the forces earmarked for the operation, both human and material – was simply impossible.

In consequence, on 15 April the initial planning document was superseded by Operational Order No 6, which became the definitive directive for the Kursk offensive. Zitadelle was to be launched 'as soon as the weather situation permits'. At the time Hitler had earmarked the start date for Zitadelle as 3 May – just eighteen days away. In his injunction that the operation 'must succeed rapidly', Hitler was indicating his awareness of the potential danger that both assault forces faced by virtue of their launching attacks from salients that were themselves vulnerable to counter strokes by the Red Army. The demand in the Operational Order – that German forces in the line to the north and south take special care to prepare strong defences to fend off Soviet attacks once Zitadelle began – is evidence of Hitler's profound awareness of the highly speculative nature of the whole enterprise. Indeed, his subsequent and oft quoted aside to General Heinz Guderian – the Inspector General of Panzer Troops – some months later, that the very notion of Zitadelle made his 'stomach turn over', is evidence enough that he knew exactly the risks he was taking.

Convinced that victory would once more attend German arms – providing Zitadelle was launched quickly – Hitler and the whole coterie of the High Command would have been horrified if they

Inspector General of Panzer Troops Heinz Guderian was always against Zitadelle.

had learnt as this early date that far from assailing a Red Army preparing to launch its own offensive, it would find itself battering against an immense force drawn up for a strategic defensive. For just three days before the release of Operational Order No:6, decisions taken in Moscow had gone far to assuring the ruin of Germany's last great offensive in Russia and setting the seal on her inevitable military defeat.

The potential of the Kursk salient for strategic exploitation had not gone unnoticed by the leader of the Soviet Union and Supreme Commander of the Red Army, Joseph Stalin. He had voiced his desire to see it used as a springboard for an early Russian offensive (as Hitler/Manstein had assumed he would) much to the consternation of his deputy, Marshal Georgi Zhukov. This had prompted him to send a telegram to Stalin in which he stated that it would not be 'expedient' to launch such an offensive. Rather the Red Army should conduct a strategic defensive within the salient and defeat what he saw as the inevitable German attack upon it. Zhukov's rationale for claiming that the Kursk bulge would be the primary, if not only, focus of German offensive intentions for the coming summer, turned on his perceptive analysis of the enemy's military weakness and the constraints that must necessarily limit his offensive options.

The decisive factor was the reduced number of infantry formations available to the Germans in consequence of their great losses over the past two years. They would be unable to disguise their true offensive intentions by employing bodies of men elsewhere, as they had done at the beginning of their 1942 summer campaign. On that occasion the concentration of a large number of such formations before Moscow had convinced Stalin and the High Command that a resumption of the attack on Moscow was the enemy's true intent, whereas the real weight of German offensive strength was deployed in the south. Zhukov also argued that given their paucity of their infantry formations, the enemy would of necessity fall back on the employment of their armoured divisions to force an early offensive decision and examination of where the bulk of them were to be found would be the best indicator of where they would attack.

Even a cursory inspection of the maps showed that the bulk of Germany's armoured divisions, including many of their elite

It was Deputy Supreme Commander Marshal Georgi Zhukov who recommended to Stalin that the Red Army defeat the German offensive by fighting a defensive battle in the Kursk salient.

formations, were deployed facing the northern and southern faces of the Kursk salient and so placed to execute the favoured German tactic of employing armoured shears to excise the position. Zhukov argued that a strategic defence should be designed that would 'impale' the still formidable resources of Germany's primary offensive arm in the East – its panzer divisions – so as to 'bleed them white'. The Head of the Red Army's Operations Sections, General Shtemenko, later articulated the massive advantage that such a strategic defensive would confer on the Russians: 'It was here, against the enemy's main concentration, that we ourselves could use our manpower and weapons to the greatest effect, particularly our big tank formations. No other sector, even if we were successful there, promised as much as the Kursk salient.'

Implicit in Shtemenko's observation and indeed in Zhukov's submission of 8 April, was the recognition and acceptance of the continuing superiority of German armoured formations when engaged in wide-ranging mobile operations. Circumstances however had conspired to force the Germans into embracing an offensive strategy that must, in the short term, negate this crucial advantage and require them to employ their armour in a fashion that played directly to the Red Army's strength and expertise in defensive operations. The lead-time given to the Red Army to prepare the salient to receive the German offensive would permit them to employ their imaginative expertise to the full in transforming the battlefield into a redoubt by July. Once battle was joined and the Soviets were convinced that their defences had achieved their purpose of wearing down the German assault forces, the second phase of their strategy would begin. The Red Army would initiate wide-ranging, pre-arranged counteroffensives to effect the complete destruction of the enemy formations.

A decision was reached with Stalin provisionally accepting the case to embrace a strategic defence. Nonetheless, as insurance should the German offensive succeed – he also allocated defensive tasks to the Bryansk Front and the South-Western and Southern Fronts. However, Stalin's most important decision came a few weeks

Joseph Stalin, Supreme Commander of the Red Army, with two of the architects of the plan to defeat the Kursk offensive; Marshal Georgi Zhukov (centre), deputy supreme commander of the Red Army and General Vasilevsky, the Chief of the Soviet General Staff.

later when he ordered the creation of the Steppe Military District (renamed Steppe Front on 10 July). This was allocated to the Stavka reserve and would constitute the largest such formation assembled by the Red Army during the course of the war. By late April, the forces in the Steppe Military District, built around the nucleus of the Fifth Guards Tank Army, comprised a further five armies, one air army and six tank and mechanised corps. In total, some 570,000 men deployed as far north as Orel and southward through to Vorishilovgrad. These forces were thus stationed across all possible axes of eastward advance the Germans could take in the event of the collapse of the Soviet defence of the salient.

The start of the second, counter offensive phase, would be signalled by the launch of Operation *Kutuzov* by the combined forces

INTEL

Stalin was not wholly dependent on the say-so of his deputy in making up his mind. Unbeknownst to Zhukov, the Soviet leader was in possession of intelligence from two other sources that supported his deputy's case. There was 'sanitised' information provided by the British from their reading of German Enigma traffic carried out by their 'ULTRA' secret SIGINT operation at Bletchley Park in England, and more from a Soviet spy ring based in Switzerland code-named 'Lucy' that seemed to have an informant very close to the High Command in Germany. Both sources agreed that the Kursk salient was to be the focus of the forthcoming German offensive. The Russians were also receiving unsanitised Enigma intercepts from their agent John Cairncross, who worked in Bletchley Park. He drove down to London every weekend and handed over the SIGINT Intel to his handler.

of the Central, Western and Bryansk Fronts. This operation was to be directed against the formations of the misnamed 2nd Panzer Army (it had no panzer divisions) defending the Orel salient to the rear of Ninth Army – the German formation charged with offensive operations in the north of the Kursk salient during *Zitadelle* – and was to be launched even as it was still involved in its assault upon it. Stavka would order the shift from defence to counter-offence in consultation with its representatives on the spot once it was certain that the German assault had been ground down and halted by the Central Front and that all enemy formations had been committed.

Unlike *Kutuzov*, wherein all planning took place prior to the operations to contain *Zitadelle*, the counter offensive in the south of the bulge, which would employ the forces of the Voronezh and Steppe Fronts, was not planned in any detail before the German offensive. Indeed, the Soviets assumed that the exact timing and form of *Polkovodets Rumyantsev*, as it was subsequently designated, would depend upon the outcome of the defensive battle with the forces of

Army Group South. Nonetheless, it was understood that whenever *Rumyantsev* was launched, it would be in tandem with diversionary offensives undertaken on the South and South-Western Fronts, the purpose of which would be to force the Germans to detach their panzer divisions southward to protect the Donbass. These offensives were to contribute in a profound fashion to the undoing of Army Group South's position by the end of the summer.

The fruits of this vast, complex and wide-ranging operation could not be doubted. Victory over the *Ostheer* in the summer would irrevocably lead to the final passing of the military initiative on the Eastern Front to the Red Army and with it, in the longer term, and after much further fighting, the triumph of the Soviet Union in this greatest and cruellest of all wars against Nazi Germany.

The Battlefield

The Kursk salient was demarcated by the towns of Orel to the north and Belgorod to the south with the land between known as the Central Russian ridge. Although implying a hilly upland even at its highest point the land is no more than 300 metres above sea level. In general, the area is a wide plain characterised by gently rolling hills and plateaus.

Much of this terrain is punctuated by ancient low burial mounds which would provide vantage points to observe enemy movements and thus would become the focus of intense fighting. Bisecting the terrain of the salient were numerous deep gorges known as *balkas* cut by rivers and streams such as the Oka, Sym, Psel and Pena. As these run mainly east-west, they straddled the German north-south line of advance. These *balkas* were almost always below the line of sight and cannot be seen until reached and were employed by the Soviets to mask and station their forces.

For Ninth Army, the dominating feature of their battlefield was the Olkhovatka heights which lay between 12 and 15 kilometres to the south of the German start line. Whilst not especially high, they overlooked the grounds to the north, thus providing the Soviets with a superb view of the terrain across which the Germans had to advance. The seizure of these heights was the primary objective of Model's forces and once achieved, would unlock the Soviet defences in the north of the salient.

Although able to employ the forests to assemble their forces to the north of their start line, once Ninth Army began its advance towards the heights and south-eastward towards MaloArchangelsk, it would move over ground pocked by collective farms and villages and numerous stands and copses of silver birch that broke up the terrain. Many villages followed the lines of *balkas* with their fields being on the steppe. Others, such as Ponyri, had grown up alongside the Orel–Kursk railway line and as collecting points for local produce and had acquired structures such as grain silos and brick/concrete buildings.

An analysis of the terrain in the south of the salient was contained in a report by the *Grossdeutschland* division when evaluating the land over which it and the SS Panzer Corps would have to advance. It stated that it was

> … a broad, gently undulating plain broken by numerous valleys but also steep sided ravines called *balkas*. These offered cover but could also be obstacles. Between them lay randomly distributed villages situated on hills, but also in valleys. The Pena river was a rather fast-flowing stream. The rising hills to the north favoured the defender. Vast grain fields covered the countryside and restricted the view. The hollows and streambeds as well as the banks of the Pena were marshy. While the terrain was less than ideal tank country, it was also not tank-proof but could be easily fortified. Tanks and armoured vehicles could easily move on the slopes or ridgelines.

For Army Detachment Kempf, the lie of the land was more problematic. Having crossed the Donets, which at Belgorod could reach up to 60 metres in width, the German forces' intention was to anchor their eastern flank, pivot through 90 degrees and drive north. From the outset, both to the fore and on their right, the German forces would be confronted by extensive forest that edged onto the river lowland that had been heavily fortified by the Soviets. The Soviet plan to contain the advance of III Panzer Corps armour and prevent it breaking out into open country had seen the rolling hills between the forest edge and the Donets provided with extensive fortifications.

Where possible, the Germans intended to use whatever roads could be secured although none in the salient were metalled and thus all-weather. Those depicted on maps were wide tracks, the black earth of which was compacted into a hard surface by the weight of the traffic moving along them. The onset of rain radically changed the consistency, turning it to mud that clung to the boots of soldiers and packed suspension units of tanks. Experience in Russia had shown how mud could unpick even the best laid offensive plan.

Nor was this just an occasional event in the high summer of central Russia, for the humidity and cloud cover over the area of the salient during the July is high and extensive. Heavy rainfall and thunderstorms cause flash floods in the *balkas*, rapidly saturating the heavy soil, in consequence of which many low-lying areas in the ravines became marshy and formed barriers to the passage of armoured vehicles.

It was over this terrain that the Battle of Kursk would be fought and its conduct would be in the hands of the following operating in their respective roles as Army Group, Army, Corps and Front level commanders.

THE ARMIES

The Commanders

The German Commanders

Panzer Ausf D of Panzer Abteilung 52 attached to 48th Panzer Corps serving with 4th Panzer Army.

Generalfeldmarschall Erich von Manstein (1887–1973), Commander of Army Group South

Regarded by many as the finest of all of Germany's senior commanders, Erich von Manstein commanded Army Group South during *Zitadelle* and oversaw the operation in the south of the salient. He was recognised early on in his career as possessing a remarkable grasp of strategy. Manstein was responsible for the plan behind the German invasion of France in 1940. Although not a tank general, he nonetheless demonstrated a consummate grasp of the principles of mobile warfare when commanding the 56th Panzer Corps during the invasion of Russia. Appointed commander of 11th Army in the Crimea, Hitler made him a Field Marshal after the capture of Sevastapol in July 1942. He was then given command of Army Group Don and led an abortive attempt to relieve Sixth Army in Stalingrad. Thereafter, he masterminded the German retreat from the Caucasus and managed, in March 1943, to retrieve and stabilize the situation by a counteroffensive victory at Kharkov. By that date, he had been made Commander of Army Group South. After Kursk, relations between Hitler and Manstein steadily declined

and in March 1944, having presented him with the Swords to his Knights Cross, the Führer dismissed him from his command.

Generalfeldmarschall Erich von Manstein.

Colonel-General Hermann Hoth (1885–1971), Commander of 4th Panzer Army

Affectionately known as 'Papa', the diminutive Hermann Hoth was promoted to Major-General and divisional commander in 1935. He took command of XV Motorised Corps and led it in the Polish campaign. Raised to full General in July 1940, it was during *Barbarossa*, when he commanded 3rd Panzer Corps as part of Army Group Centre, that he came to prominence. In October, he took command of 17th Army and thence 4th Panzer Army in 1942. He led this formation into the suburbs of Stalingrad and also as the centrepiece of the abortive attempt to relieve the encircled Sixth Army in the city in December. For the Kursk offensive, 4th Panzer Army provided the primary striking force in the southern sector of the salient. In its aftermath, he continued to command 4th Panzer Army in its retreat westward until relieved by Hitler in November.

Colonel-General Hermann Hoth.

General of Panzer Troops Werner Kempf (1886–1969), Commander of Army Detachment Kempf

Werner Kempf began his Second World War career as Generalmajor and the commander of Panzer Division 'Kempf' in the invasion of Poland. He succeeded to the command of the 6th Panzer Division, leading it in the invasion of France. He was promoted thereafter to Generalleutnant and was awarded the Knights Cross. On 6 January 1941, he was appointed commander of 48th Panzer Corps and on 1 April General der Panzer Truppen. Following Hitler's dismissal of General Lanz in February 1943, he appointed Kempf to take the latter's place with his command being known as Army Detachment Kempf and served at Kursk. From May to September 1944, he commanded the Wehrmacht in the Baltic and was then transferred to the leadership reserve.

General of Panzer Troops Werner Kempf.

Generalfeldmarschall Gunther von Kluge (1882–1944), Commander of Army Group Centre

Assuming the post of Commander of Army Group Centre in December 1941 after Hitler sacked his predecessor, von Kluge was to remain in post until he was badly injured in October 1943. Kluge had commanded the Fourth Army in Poland, and led the Sixth in the Battle for France, for which he was rewarded by being promoted to Field Marshal. He commanded Fourth Army as part of Army Group Centre under the command of Field Marshal von Bock during *Barbarossa*. He oversaw the weathering of a number of Soviet offensives directed towards the destruction of his command and though he was unwilling to aid von Manstein using his own mobile forces to destroy the Kursk salient in March, he was a strong and unrelenting supported of *Zitadelle*. He took his own life in August 1944, when he was recalled to Berlin from his role as commander of German forces in Normandy on suspicion he had been involved in the 20 July Bomb Plot to kill Hitler.

Generalfeldmarschall Gunther von Kluge.

Colonel-General Walter Model (1891–1945), Commander of Ninth Army

Hitler was to call Model '*mein bester FeldMarschall*'. His wartime career began in the rank of Generalmajor serving as Chief of Staff to IV Corps in Poland and Sixteenth Army in the French Campaign. He was appointed to command of 3rd Panzer Division in November 1940. Allocated to Second Panzer Group for Barbarossa, Model ruthlessly drove his well-trained division and it had reached the Dnieper by 4 July. It was in the winter of 1941–42 that he emerged as a defensive specialist. In January, he was appointed to command Ninth Army. It was then that he came to Hitler's notice. In the winter of 42/43, he defeated Zhukov's massive attempt to destroy the Rzhev salient. With the decision to abandon the salient so as to release Ninth Army for offensive operations in the summer, Model conducted an extremely successful withdrawal in March 1943. Ninth Army was allocated the responsibility for attacking the north of the salient in Operation *Zitadelle*. Following the failure of *Zitadelle*, his reputation survived and grew as he conducted successful defensive operations. He was entrusted with greater command responsibility by Hitler, who made him a Field Marshal in 1944. Model was employed on both the Eastern and Western Fronts in

effect as the 'Führer's fireman' from July 1944. He committed suicide on 21 April 1945.

Colonel-General Walter Model.

The Soviet Commanders

Army General Konstantin K. Rokossovsky (1896–1968), Commander of the Central Front

It was his Polish origins that had led to the arrest, imprisonment and torture of Rokossovsky as a spy in 1937. Until then, he had risen through the ranks of the Red Army and had in the early thirties even commanded Zhukov. In 1940, he was rehabilitated and released from prison – albeit minus nine teeth and his fingernails – and appointed Colonel. With the onset of *Barbarossa* he was commander of the 9th Mechanised Corps and in September, Stalin appointed him commander of 16th Army – the first composed entirely of soldiers serving in penal battalions. His career flourished, and as commander of the Don Front, led the north wing in the offensive that encircled Sixth Army in Stalingrad at the end of November 1942. Appointed commander of the Central Front he oversaw the construction of the defences, the strategy and the successful operations of the Soviet forces in the north of the Kursk salient. Thereafter he held senior commands, being promoted Marshal in 1944. In November he was made commander of the 2nd Belorussian Front. At the end of April 1945 his Front joined up with the forces of Montgomery in northern Germany. He had a significant post-war career.

Army General Konstantin K. Rokossovsky.

Army General Nikolai F. Vatutin (1901–1944), Commander of the Voronezh Front

Nikolai Vatutin was regarded as one of the brightest of the younger cadre of commanders to emerge in the first years of the war. Prior to the German invasion he had held mainly staff posts and lacked command experience. At the end of June 1941 he was appointed as CofS of the North Western Front. In January 1942, he achieved the first encirclement of enemy forces by trapping two German corps in Demyansk. Between May and July he served as Deputy Chief of the General Staff after which Stalin despatched him as Stavka representative to the Bryansk Front. This was then renamed the Voronezh Front and Vatutin was appointed its commander. In late September he was transferred and given command of the new South-western Front and played a major role in the planning and execution of the defeat of Sixth Army in Stalingrad. Thereafter, he helped push the Germans back into the western Ukraine but his overextended forces were defeated by Manstein in his counteroffensive in February/March 1943. Stalin promoted him to the rank of Army General and gave him command of the Voronezh Front at the end of March. He then oversaw the construction of the defences in the south of the salient. His fondness for attack saw him try and convince Stalin on a few occasions before July to attack the Germans rather than await their offensive. He died in March 1944 following wounds received in an attack by a Ukrainian nationalist force.

Army General Nikolai F. Vatutin.

Colonel-General Ivan S. Konev (1897–1973), Commander of the Steppe Military District (Steppe Front from 9 July)

When war broke out in June 1941 Konev had already held a number of high military commands and was appointed to command the 19th Army. He played a major role in the counteroffensive before Moscow as commander of the Kalinin Front for which he was promoted to Colonel-General. In August 1942, he assumed command of the Western Front and in March 1943, the Northwestern Front. With Stalin's decision to create the Steppe Reserve – the largest such formation created by the Red Army during the war – Konev was moved once more to take command of this massive formation. Renamed the Steppe Front, Konev was involved in the major counteroffensive operations that followed after the German defeat at Kursk, including the final recapture of Kharkov and the crossing of the river Dnieper. Renamed once more as the 2nd Ukrainian Front, Konev was involved in Red Army offensive operations in command of this formation through to war's end including the Red Army's last major operation of the conflict, the capture of Prague at the beginning of May 1945. He and Zhukov were seen by others and saw themselves as rivals. He remained a high-profile figure post-war and commanded Soviet forces in the suppression of the Hungarian Uprising in 1956.

Colonel General Ivan S. Konev.

The Soldiers

The German Army

Unsurprisingly German troops wore a variety of uniform during the course of the battle. While some *landsers* were still to be seen in *feldgrau*, the more common summer wear was the M1940 reed-green fatigue twill tunic with others dressed in the 1942 pullover style cotton shirt as outer clothing. The newer M1942 reed-green herringbone twill tunic with similar colour trousers was only appearing in quantity by the time of Kursk. Becoming more common by this date were lace-up ankle boots that were replacing the leather jackboot. In combat, infantry wore the M1935 steel helmet in its standard greenish-grey colour to which could be added webbing or a camouflage cover. A variety of Y-straps were employed attached to the belt to which were attached leather pouches carrying ammunition/magazines for either the Kar98 rifle or MP 38/40 machine pistol. Percussion and stick grenades were carried on the belt. When so armed, a pistol holder would be on this belt. The bayonet and an entrenching tool were worn behind the left hip. A gas mask container was carried on a diagonal slung strap. Although there were regulations to be adhered too, the strain on supply saw a variety of mix and match amongst officers and other ranks in all arms so it is impossible to define a prescribed uniform. Many tank crewmen still wore the distinctive black tunic top and trousers whilst others used just the black top with reed-green panzer fatigue trousers.

Waffen SS troops wore much of the same weaponry and variety of uniform as did the *Heer*, although their *infanterie* and *panzer grenadiere* were easily distinguishable by their camouflage smocks and helmet covers.

Senior German officers still had reason to believe that the effectiveness and quality of their troops remained superior to those of the enemy in the summer of 1943. But if the Red Army was a

BOOTS ON THE GROUND

In 1943, the OKH had been obliged to introduce a new divisional structure that was governed by the reality of declining manpower. Whereas in 1939, an infantry division had an establishment of 17,734 men, this now fell to just 12,772 troops. Although retaining the same structure of three infantry regiments and one of artillery, each was reduced to just two battalions of 700 men. Even then, this was a paper establishment because such was the scale of losses that few divisions even possessed this level of manpower. Even Ninth Army, in the days before the launch of *Zitadelle*, reflected this reality. Only one of Model's infantry divisions was described as being of the 'highest offensive level' with another four being fit for only 'limited offensive action'.

very different institution from that of two summers before, the same was also true of the Wehrmacht. Whereas the former was demonstrating improvements in all aspects of its performance, the latter was on a downward spiral, it was a lesser force than it had been when it invaded the Soviet Union in June 1941.

Whilst Kursk is forever linked with the clash of armour, the deterioration of the German Army is best exemplified by the state of its primary arm – the infantry. This appears to be paradoxical inasmuch as there were 51 more infantry divisions in service in 1943 than two years before, when at the launch of *Barbarossa*, the *Heer* was fielding 175 divisions. This expansion was illusory; as we have already seen, the great losses in the infantry arm since 1941 had both substantially reduced divisional establishments and also seen a decline in the quality of replacements.

The Red Army

Historically, the Russian soldier has always been known as incredibly hardy and in the Second World War the German experience of the Red Army soldiery was no different. Although poorly trained compared to the German *landser*, the ordinary Soviet ranker at Kursk functioned within a ferociously hard and disciplined structure. He (and she) was nonetheless patriotic, stubborn, existing on little and prepared to die in the service of the *Rodina* (motherland) – which in this battle they were to do in their thousands.

The most apparent signal of the many changes affecting the Red Army in 1943 was the reintroduction of the pre-revolutionary shoulder boards and coloured piping representing different arms of service. Stalin was prepared to eschew ideology to foster a genuine sense of patriotism in the decision to reach back to the army of the old regime and its military heroes for new awards. Alongside this went the reduction in the powers of the political commissar who no longer had the power to override the professional military.

The basic component of the field uniform was the *gymnastiorka* – a simple blouse that looked like that worn by most peasants. Of the two issues, that worn by infantry at Kursk would have been for the summer and was made of cotton. Some pictures from the battle show soldiers wearing the padded *telgroika* jacket. By 1942, acute shortages of materials and dyes would have seen a profusion of hues of khaki and a wide variation in the quality of the clothing. Officers also wore the blouse. Both rankers and officers wore *shovari*, which resembled riding trousers and flared from the hip. A black belt was worn – rankers with an ordinary buckle whereas officers wore a Sam Browne belt and a more ornate brass buckle stamped with a Soviet Star. Footwear again was dependent on rank – officers wore black leather boots while ordinary ranks had low boots with puttees or high boots of lesser quality. Rain capes wear also issued and *razvedchik* troops wore camouflage smocks coloured khaki and black. Many soldiers wore their greatcoats even in high summer, especially at night. Headwear was primarily the steel helmet but many soldiers photographed in the battle are wearing khaki side caps. As with German soldiers, there were many variations that were a product of supply problems.

The Kit

The German Army

It was hoped that the introduction of many more and improved automatic weapons would serve to raise the volume and effectiveness of the firepower of the infantry in compensation for its smaller manpower level. Greater numbers of MP40 machine pistols were issued alongside the new MG42 heavy machine gun that supplemented the older MG34. Heavier mortars – the largest being the 120mm sGrW, which had been copied from a Soviet weapon of the same calibre – was serving alongside larger numbers of the 75mm Pak 40 anti-tank guns.

Such had been the losses in artillery in the previous two years that German forces at Kursk found themselves heavily outnumbered by the Red Army in this arm. The types of artillery pieces in service were no different than those with which the German Army went to war in 1939, nor was their organisation. In addition to conventional artillery there were the *Neberlwerfer Abteilungen* equipped with multi-barrelled rocket mortars as well as the new self-propelled artillery. Although these served in small numbers with panzer divisions, these saw standard artillery pieces mounted on full tracked chassis. The *Wespe* mounted the 105mm light field howitzer on a modified Panzer II chassis, the *Grille* mounted the 150mm infantry gun on an adapted Panzer 38(t) chassis and the 150mm heavy field Howitzer was mounted on a stretched Panzer III/IV chassis and named *Hummel*. All three saw service at Kursk for the first time.

The Panzer Divisions

It was the panzers operating en masse at Kursk that the Germans were reliant upon to be the primary instrument of the rapid victory demanded by Hitler. By the launch of *Zitadelle*, 70 per cent of the total armour available to the *Ostheer* had been allocated to the

PAPER TIGERS

Not one of the German army tank divisions deployed the paper strength of the two-battalion regiment of 160 panzers. Other than the *Grossdeutschland* division and the three panzer grenadier divisions of II SS Panzer Corps, whose tank establishments were higher in consequence of their elite status, the panzer divisions disposed of an average of just 70 machines for the battle. Between the beginning of April and 22 June, 699 panzers and 318 assault guns were despatched eastward.

offensive. 85 per cent of the tanks and assault guns committed were of Panzer III, IV and StuG IIIs with the remainder comprising the Tigers, Panthers, Ferdinands and Brummbärs.

To ensure that the panzer and assault gun formations earmarked for *Zitadelle* were equipped for the task, the bulk of the rising numbers of both, in addition to the totally new designs leaving the production lines, were allocated to service the offensive.

Panzer Mark III

The second most numerous panzer employed at Kursk was already being phased out of production in Germany. The limitations in the armour and firepower of the 22-ton Panzer III had been rudely exposed by encounters with the Red Army's superior T-34 and KV tanks in the early days of *Barbarossa*. Although up-gunned with a longer 50mm L/60 gun, it remained deficient. Nonetheless, 668 served in the battle.

Panzer Mark IV

Assuming the role of the Mark III as the main tank in the panzer divisions was the 25-ton Panzer IV, whose turret ring was wide enough for it to be up-gunned with the long barrelled 75mm L/43 and L/48 weapons. While 1942 production of this type was still low, by 1943 it had risen to take the place of the Panzer III as the primary

The Panzer Mark III was obsolete by the time of Kursk but many served in the battle. This image shows the side skirts (schurzen) worn by many in the battle.

The most numerous German tank in the battle was the Panzer IV. This example is a Model G, without schurzen.

tank employed by the panzer divisions. 702 Mark IVs were available on 5 July.

Panzer Mark VI: Tiger

Representing a gun/armour combination which at the time of Kursk the Red Army could not match, the 57-ton Tiger I heavy tank had already proven itself a formidable tank killer. Its 88mm gun could penetrate all Soviet tanks. Its frontal armour was impervious at battle ranges to all Soviet anti-tank guns. Tiger tanks were allocated to special heavy tank battalions although just two of these – *schwere Panzer Abteilungen* 503 and 505 – served at Kursk, the three Waffen SS Panzer Grenadier divisions of the II SS Panzer Corps each fielded their own Tiger companies, as did the elite army division *Grossdeutschland*. 147 Tiger Is would see action at Kursk with 102 of those serving in the south of the salient.

The Tiger I was the most powerful panzer to serve at Kursk.

The battle winner for Hitler: the new Panther medium tank seen loading up for transport to Russia to see service for the first time at Kursk.

Panzer Mark V: Panther

Seeing service for the first time in the offensive was the 44-ton Panzerkampfwagen V Panther medium tank. Arising out of the need for a tank that could both defeat and be superior to the Russian KV and T-34, it drew on the latter in its use of sloped armour. Although its frontal armour was as heavy as that of the Tiger, that of its flanks was thinner. It mounted a 75mm L/70 high velocity gun that could take out a T-34 at long range. Its Achilles heel, due to premature commitment to combat, was its mechanical unreliability with a tendency for its engine to catch fire. Nonetheless, it took a heavy toll of Soviet tanks in the battle even though deemed to have been less than a success. 200 Panthers were allocated to the offensive.

Assault Gun: Sturmgeschutz III

The third most numerous type of German AFV at Kursk was a turret-less assault gun – the 23-ton *Sturmgeschutz* (abbreviated to StuG) – based on the Panzer III chassis and mounting the same

The Sturmgeschutz III – assault gun, or StuG. By summer 1943 it had acquired a reputation as a formidable tank killer.

75mm gun as the Panzer IV. Other than *Grossdeutschland* and the Waffen SS divisions which had their own organic StuG units, all others were manned by members of the artillery and operated in StuG battalions (*Abteilungen*) of 31 machines. The bulk of these were attached to a panzer division or a corps for the offensive. 463 StuGs, including those mounting the 105mm howitzer for infantry support, were available for the offensive.

Assault Gun with 88mm PaK 43: Sturmgeschutz Ferdinand

Serving only with Ninth Army were 90 Ferdinand assault gun/ heavy tank destroyers equipping two out of three battalions that formed PanzerJäger Regiment 656. Mounting an immensely powerful 88mm PaK 43 cannon, this machine was named for its designer Dr Ferdinand Porsche. Very thickly armoured and extremely heavy – weighting in at some 65 tons – Hitler expected much of it. But it lacked a machine gun for close-in defence and its novel electric drive – with each track being driven by a separate motor – was complex and prone to breakdown. Its weight made recovery difficult.

A line-up of the new heavyweight Ferdinand heavy assault gun before the battle; Hitler expected much of this machine. It only operated with Ninth Army.

Assault Infantry Gun: Sturmpanzer Brummbär

The third battalion of Panzerjäger Regiment 656 was also equipped with a new type – the 45 Brummbären of Sturm-Panzer 216. Employing a Panzer IV chassis this assault tank mounted a 150mm heavy infantry howitzer in a fixed, heavily armoured superstructure. The 28-ton Brummbär had also been built without a machine gun for close-in defence that would have enabled them to deal with Soviet tank hunting teams.

SPWs

Although not panzers, the one and three-ton half-track SPWs carried the panzer grenadiers that operated with the panzers and played a major role in German mobile warfare. They were also employed in many other roles and were vital components of the all-arms combat formations employed by them.

GERMAN ARMOUR FOR *ZITADELLE*

Tank/StuG/Pjag/SPG Strength of 4th Panzer Army –
5/7/1943: 1153
Tank/StuG/Pjag/SPG Strength of III Panzer Corps –
5/7/1943: 358
Tank/StuG/Pjag/SPG Strength of Ninth Army – 5/7/1943:
821

The Red Army

By the summer of 1943, the armament of the infantryman had improved substantially from that of earlier years. The basic weapon was the same as that of the First World War – the 7.62 Moisin Nagant Model 1891/30 with modifications. The most common sub machine gun was the PPsh with its distinctive drum magazine and wooden stock. Standard machine gun was the 7.62mm Degtyarev *DP*, nicknamed the 'record player' because of the large circular magazine it employed. The primary infantry anti-tank weapon was the anti-tank rifle, which although regarded as passé was employed with great effectiveness in its thousands in the battle, with, for example, troopers being told to target the vision blocks on the cupolas of German tanks.

Most other, non-tank Soviet armies encountered by the Germans in the battle contained either two or three rifle corps of between seven or twelve rifle divisions, with each deploying four artillery regiments equipped with 152mm heavy guns, 76mm divisional guns, 37mm AA guns and 122mm mortars. This gave each Army 1250 guns and mortars. These could be augmented at the behest of the Stavka to 2700 pieces. The measure of the growth of the size of these formations was that they were raised from 40,000 to 130,000 men.

In the absence of machines such as the German SPW to carry troops to operate alongside tanks, infantry had to be carried into

UNCLE SAM'S WHEELS

'I recorded a conversation with a Russian correspondent who had just been to Kursk. He said the Russian equipment there was truly stupendous; he had never seen anything like it. What was going to make a big difference this summer was the enormous number of American trucks; these were going to increase Russian mobility to an enormous degree. The Russian soldiers were finding them excellent.'

Alexander Werth

battle by the *desant* method. Red Army infantry would mount the hull of a tank and then hold on to the railings that had been welded onto the hull and turret for this purpose. Unwilling to produce specialist machines like the German infantry half-tracks at the expense of tanks, it was only in 1942 and especially 1943, with the supply of many thousands of lorries from the US, that the Red Army began to acquire a degree of mobility that matched the *Ostheer.* The battle of Kursk witnessed the first massed employment of these machines.

The Soviet artillery arm saw a formidable expansion in its destructive capabilities. The role of artillery had always had a special place in Red Army doctrine and the changes introduced in the first half of 1943 saw the new formations added to the order of battle to play an integral role. The primary artillery formation at the end of 1942 was the division, of which there were eleven, each fielding a maximum of 168 guns and mortars. In the months prior to Kursk a new formation was introduced, the purpose of which was apparent from its title. The Penetration Division could deploy 356 guns and mortars and when two were combined with a guard's mortar division to form an Artillery Penetration Corps, it could deploy unprecedented firepower of no less than 712 guns/mortars and 864 *Katyusha* launchers. A similar expansion and organisational change occurred with anti-tank artillery when the artillery destroyer regiments, of which there were 240 at the end of 1942, were grouped into the larger brigade five months later. By the time of Kursk, 20 tank destroyer brigades had been created, with each deploying up to a maximum of 72 anti-tank and divisional guns of 45 and 76.2mm calibre (the 57mm coming into service by Kursk) serviced by 1850 troops.

The Tank Army

By the time of Kursk, the Soviets were able to call on the influx of equipment streaming from their factories beyond the Urals and deliveries from the US and UK via Lend Lease. It was the tank formations that provided evidence that the Red Army was gearing up for massive offensive operations. The Tank Army was introduced to become the core Red Army formation with five established by order in January 1943 – all of which would be engaged within the salient and in the counteroffensive operations. Each comprised on paper two tank and one mechanised corps fielding about 800 tanks with integral artillery, *katyusha*, SP gun and other supporting regiments. The massive expansion in tank output also saw armour distributed to separate tank brigades and regiments that were increased in number and size, the latter fielding 66 T-34s and 21 T-70s. There was also a smaller number of 'heavy' KV-1 and KV-1S tanks serving in 'penetration regiments'.

One of the primary weaknesses of Soviet tanks that superior German command and control had been able to exploit was their limited number of radios. By the summer of 1943, these were far more common with large numbers of American sets delivered via Lend-Lease being fitted into T-34s, enabling formations to function with greater direction and coherence.

The high level of productivity lends strong credibility to the case that it was the Red Army that benefited in every respect from the long delay by Hitler in launching *Zitadelle*. The mass of T-34s produced between April and the end of June permitted the Soviets to build up superiority in numbers in and around the salient and mass such a huge reserve beyond it that even when large numbers were destroyed during the course of the limited German advance, those available for the counteroffensive operations were so numerous and operated over such a wide area that they overwhelmed all German attempts to contain the Red Army post-Kursk.

NUMBERS GAME

The mass-production of the T-34 and its ubiquity on the battlefield at Kursk (and beyond) came in many ways to epitomise the Soviet way of war encapsulated in a saying from Lenin, wholeheartedly endorsed by Stalin: 'Quantity has its own quality.'

By spring of 1943, 2000 T-34s were being produced a month on the production lines in the factories beyond the Urals. Life expectancy for a new T-34 at this time was about one week.

ARMS RACE

It was the appearance of the Tiger and intelligence acquired of the specifications of the new Panther that finally prompted development of a larger turret with an 85mm gun on the T-34 chassis, but this would not enter service until early 1944.

The T-34

By the summer of 1943, the T-34 had become the predominant tank in production and in service with the Red Army, with all medium tank formations being equipped with it. Although by then, the 26-ton T-34 no longer retained the technical edge over its opponents, this was compensated for by the far greater numbers of this machine available. Although the limitation of the 76.2mm main armament had been recognised in 1942, when the Germans introduced the up-gunned Stug III and Panzer IV, the decision was taken to retain the gun so as not to interfere with production. This, by early 1943, was running at 2000 tanks per month in the factories beyond the Urals.

T-70

The second most numerous tank used by the Red Army at Kursk was the T-70 light tank. Weighing 9.5 tons and manned by a crew of two it had a main armament of a 45mm gun. Many were lost in the battle and post-Kursk, the decision was taken to phase out the light tank altogether although the chassis was retained as the basis of the Su-76M SPG, which also saw service for the first in the battle.

KV-1 and KV-1S

The KV-1 heavy tank, which had made such an impression on the Germans in 1941 was a declining asset two years later. Although strongly armoured, it carried the same gun as the T-34 and cost nearly three times as much to produce. A lighter variant called the KV-1S but still mounting the same gun, had been introduced towards the end of 1942. It was this variant that was mainly encountered by the Germans at Kursk. An assault gun, designated the SU-152, was developed very quickly employing the KV-1 chassis and mounting a 152mm gun to counter the Tiger and Panthers at Kursk. Only a few saw action in the battle.

RED ARMY TANKS 5/7/1943

Central Front: 318 Tanks/SUs 9th, 19th Individual Tank Corps
600 – 2nd Tank Army
Voronezh Front: 634 Tanks/SUs – 1st Tank Army
696 Tanks/SUs – 2nd, 10th, 2nd Guards, 5th Guards Individual
Tank Corps
Steppe Front: 850 Tanks/SUs – 5th Guards
Tank Army

Few KV-1 heavy tanks saw action at Kursk. The few that did were organised into independent tank units.

THE DAYS BEFORE BATTLE

The German Plan

The plan for *Zitadelle* provided by the OKH was simple. Two large armoured assault groups were to issue forth from either neck of the salient and eliminate it by means of a pincer assault. As of 1 July, Ninth Army comprised five Corps, of which four were tasked with offensive roles. Mobile formations included six panzer and one panzer grenadier division.

Ninth Army was to break through the defences of the Central Front on a very narrow frontage of 40 kilometres between a line demarcated by the main Orel-Kursk road to the west and the railway linking the two cities to the east. Ninth Army was then to advance and meet up with the forces of Army Group South on the heights to the north of Kursk. A secondary thrust to the south-east was to be launched at the same time to capture and then anchor the eastern flank of Ninth Army on the important railway junction of MaloArchangelsk. This would then create a more coherent front line with 2nd Panzer Army, which lay to the north in the Orel salient. For Army Group South the main German effort was to be found in the southern arm of the pincer.

As of 1 July, 4th Panzer Army was deployed along a sixteen-kilometre front between Gertsovka and Belgorod. Operational

ARMY GROUP SOUTH

Forces allocated to Army Group South included nine panzer and
panzer grenadier divisions and eight infantry divisions. Of these,
six of the mobile and six of the infantry divisions had
been allocated to the two panzer corps comprising
4th Panzer Army.

Order No 6 stated that Army Group South 'will jump off with
strongly concentrated forces … break through the Prilepy-Oboyan
line and link up with attacking armies of Army Group Centre east
of Kursk.' Protection for 4th Panzer Army's eastern was allocated to
Armee Abteilung Kempf, allocated one panzer corps of three panzer
divisions and two corps of five infantry divisions. Having crossed the
river Donets, III Panzer Corps was to pivot to the north and then
advance in parallel with the II SS Panzer Corps.

Although the original documentation assumed that the
breakthrough to Oboyan would be achieved by a direct thrust that
would secure crossings over the river Psel below Oboyan, Manstein
and Hoth modified this in May. Mindful of the anticipated descent of
the Soviet Strategic Armoured Reserve on 4th Panzer Army's right
flank via the land bridge at Prokhorovka, and not believing that III
Panzer Corps, which had been earmarked in the Operational Order
to deal with this matter, was strong enough to defeat it, the plan
was re-jigged.

Abandoning the notion of a massed crossing by 4th Panzer Army
of the Psel at Oboyan, at the appropriate time when approaching
the river as if heading for the crossing, Hoth would order his two
panzer corps to swing their axis of advance from the north to
the north-east. With the SS Panzer Corps taking a lead role and
48th Panzer Corps screening its left flank, he intended the three
Waffen SS panzer grenadier divisions to confront and defeat the
Soviet Armoured Reserve in conjunction with III Panzer Corps, in
the vicinity of Prokhovoka. In the final orders issued by Hausser, he

designated the capture of the town of Prokhorovka and the securing of a crossing point over the river Psel, in the vicinity of Vasilevka, as the Corps' initial objectives.

The boundary lines between the SS Panzer Corps and III Panzer Corps were re-drawn so that the land bridge west and north-west of Prokhorovka fell within the SS Panzer Corps' jurisdiction. Having defeated the Strategic Reserve, the three SS divisions would then cross the Psel and drive north to meet up with Ninth Army, as per the original planning.

The Preparatory Period, April–5 July

Even before the end of April, the Germans had secured ample evidence derived from aerial photography of the salient that their assumptions as to Soviet intentions were in error. It was Model who personally presented the images to Hitler on 27 April and what they revealed was a mass of deep entrenchments slashing across the landscape on either neck of the salient indicating that the Red Army, far from preparing for an offensive, was digging in its forces for a defensive battle on a massive scale. In having divined German offensive intentions, the Soviets had, by their response, now undermined its very rationale. Clearly, if *Zitadelle* was still to go ahead, the Germans would have to fight a very different type of battle to the one planned.

As Hitler pondered the implications, it was apparent that whilst the political and military necessities that underpinned *Zitadelle* remained paramount, the conditions required for its successful execution were, judging by the growing strength of the enemy defences, reducing with each day. But no alternative plan acceptable lay to hand or was even conceivable in the face of German military weakness that would permit him to realise his overriding policy requirements.

What was to be done? His response was to issue the first of what was to become a series of delaying orders that would prove fatal to whatever possibility there was of *Zitadelle* succeeding. Initially, this

General Kurt Zeitzler was Chief of the Army General Staff (OKH) and had been a supporter of Zitadelle but wanted an early launch. By June he was voicing doubts about its validity.

was of two days, pushing the start date back to 5 May. Then, on 30 April, another, four days to 9 May. In consequence, a sense of uncertainty began to grip the German High Command. To address the issue and canvas the opinion of the senior commanders involved, Hitler summoned them to a conference in Munich on 4 May. The views they expressed ranged from cancellation on the one hand to immediate execution on the other. Manstein and Zeitzler fell into the latter camp, the former warning that to delay its launch further would risk the possibility that *Zitadelle* might coincide with Allied landings in southern Europe; a prescient observation, given that all Axis forces in the Tunis bridgehead surrendered to the Americans and British just eight days later.

Nonetheless, on the day after the conference Hitler ordered the offensive delayed until 12 June. Unwilling to cancel, the German leader now turned to the panacea of technology to resolve the matter. He argued that the five-week delay would not only permit the armoured divisions to be reinforced with more of the older, up-gunned panzers but also with further Tigers and assault guns, and especially the new Ferdinand and Panther.

Hitler had come to view the new, and on paper, superior Panther medium tank, as the 'battle winner'. Despite his enthusiasm, this new weapon was very immature and far from combat-ready as Guderian spelt out to him in a meeting in Berlin on 10 May. The Inspector of Armoured Troops reported that many of those produced were being hastily rebuilt in order to iron out their many teething problems and six weeks would not be enough to see them cured.

So it proved. And as the delay stretched seemingly ever on, prompted by the need to accommodate yet further remedial work on the Panther and perhaps also to permit Hitler to keep a weather eye on developments in Italy, the time gifted to the Red Army by the Germans let it employ all of its expertise, imagination and skill in transforming the Kursk salient into one of the most lethal fortified positions ever created.

The Citadel

That the purpose of the first phase of the defensive-offensive strategy adopted by the Stavka turned on the destruction, through attrition, of the armoured formations of the German Army committed to *Zitadelle* was apparent from the nature and scale of the defensive system they were creating within the salient. Its rigidity was intentional: its priority being to enmesh the panzers in a dense web of fortifications, so negating their mobility and capacity for effective command and control – the trump card of the *Panzerwaffe* in all of their prior operations on the Eastern Front. The panzers would thus be rendered vulnerable to destruction, primarily by artillery, but also to the other varied array of weapons deployed by the Red Army. The Red Army was engaged in the process of engineering the Kursk salient into one vast tank killing ground. Once sure they had bled the German mobile forces white and determined that all enemy reserves had been committed, the Soviets would then move to the second phase of their plan and launch their own counteroffensives. This would permit them to exploit their numerical superiority over what they assumed would be a severely weakened German panzer force.

Although the Red Army had begun construction of defensive lines within the salient even before the end of March, it was Stalin's decision of 12 April to embrace a strategic defensive that prompted the creation of the sophisticated system that would transform the bulge into a veritable citadel by July. The whole defensive system within and behind the salient was based upon eight deeply echeloned defensive zones, each comprising parallel multiple trench lines and fortifications extending rearwards to a distance of no less than 100 miles. Of these, only the first five were constructed within the salient. The remainder were built by the Steppe Reserve to straddle the neck and bulge and were echeloned eastward. The Soviet intention was to contain the German assault within the initial defensive zones of the 13th Army on the Central Front facing Ninth Army in the north and the 6th and 7th Guards Armies of the Voronezh Front. It was here that they were strongest with every position suborned to the needs of the anti-tank defence.

The first defensive zone extended from the front line rearwards to a depth of three miles and comprised five parallel lines of deep entrenchments. The forward edge was protected by very deep barbed wire fences, wide ditches, huge fields of anti-tank and anti-personnel mines, steel anti-tank teeth and local streams and rivers

Operation Zitadelle 1943

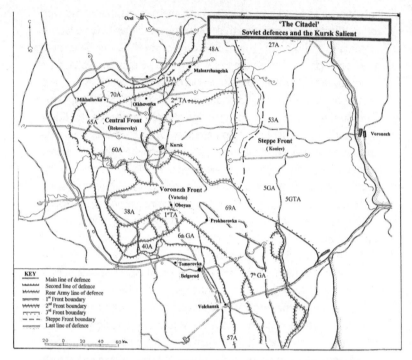

The disposition of the Red Army's defensive lines in and beyond the Kursk salient, and deployment of its Front forces for the Battle of Kursk.

dammed to flood the terrain. As the Germans attempted to breach this zone they would be under very heavy artillery which had been already ranged in. It was artillery, in all its forms, upon which the Soviets were depending to blunt the enemy's offensive drive. Indeed, post battle analysis would reveal that the greatest loss of panzers would be to the 'Soviet God of War'.

Once enmeshed within the defensive zone, the panzers and their supporting infantry, be they on foot or mounted in SPWs, would find themselves ensnared amidst a very sophisticated web of fortifications based upon a chequerboard arrangement of strongly constructed, mutually supportive and carefully disguised anti-tank strongpoints. These were disposed to cover the possible axes of the German tank formations with a density of about eight per kilometre. Each contained some five 45mm or 76mm divisional guns and 14.5mm anti-tank rifles, with their respective gunners supported by sappers and infantry with automatic weapons. On the Voronezh Front, 6th Guards Army constructed eighteen of these in its first line of defence with a further ten in its second, deployed to screen approaches to the river Psel and the town of Oboyan. In all, nearly 100 of these heavily fortified positions were created in Vatutin's command. At least 27, cleverly integrated into and deployed amid the inhospitable terrain to the east of the Donets by 7th Guards Army, would prove instrumental in delaying the progress of III Panzer Corps, confounding the German timetable in the south of the salient.

The Soviet assumption that the German assault in the north would be directed primarily against 13th Army had seen the construction of an even higher concentration of anti-tank strong points in a sector some 32 kilometres long and just a little less in depth. It is therefore not surprising that Model's forces were to find progress so difficult and costly, when in the first of the Soviet defence lines to be traversed there were no fewer than 44 of these strong points equipped with 204 guns defended by 4 rifle divisions. Nor were the second and third lines any easier with 160 guns in the former defended by three rifle divisions and a further 342 guns deployed throughout the 60 positions held by five rifle divisions in the latter.

The 6000 anti-tank guns deployed in the salient averaged out to approximately eleven per kilometre of front. However, in those sectors of the Central and Voronezh Fronts which were assumed to be those most directly threatened by the German assault, the number was significantly higher, reaching a density of twelve to fifteen for each kilometre, with these totals being substantially augmented during the course of the battle. That being said, the most numerous weapon employed in this role – the 45mm anti-tank gun – whilst able to penetrate the side armour of the Panzers III and IV, could not defeat the increased frontal armour of the upgraded variants of these designs; let alone that of the more heavily protected 'cat' family and the Ferdinand. The second most numerous gun employed in the anti-tank defence – the 76mm field gun – also could not deal with the frontal-armour of the newer German machines. Although a more effective weapon in this role, the new ZIS-2 57mm gun was only available in small numbers. To neutralise this significant disadvantage as much as possible Russian gunners were drilled to hold their fire to the very last moment to ensure a kill. It was hoped that by way of compensation the extremely effective camouflage employed to disguise the fixed positions would serve to protect the anti-guns and their crews so they could fire before being spotted by the panzers. The numerous trench lines linking the bunkers were themselves protected by barbed wire stockades, further tank ditches, numerous camouflaged machine gun nests and other obstacles. On some sectors T-34 and KV-1 tanks were dug in so only their turrets showed while many other pre-dug positions were available to be used in this way once the battle began.

Vast minefields had been 'sown' as early as April and the work continued during the offensive itself. These were not disposed in a haphazard fashion but carefully laid so as to forcibly channel the paths of the advancing panzers to would reveal their more vulnerable flanks to the pre-positioned anti-tank guns. By way of example just in the sector of 40th Army of the Voronezh Front no fewer than 50,032 tank mines, 70,994 infantry mines and 6377 large calibre shells dug into the ground and fused to act as mine barriers were laid. Roads and bridges were secured with delayed action mines, Most of the mines were placed in front of the positions taken up by the Army in the main defensive belt.

Across the 60km frontage of 6th Guards Army, upon which the full weight of Hoth's 4th Panzer Army would eventually fall, 69,998 anti-tank and 64,340 anti-personnel mines were laid in the first defensive belt alone, with a further 20,200 anti-tank and 9097 anti-personnel in the second. To the south-east, Army Detachment Kempf would discover to its cost the effect of the heavy minefields laid by Seventh Guards Army, where approximately 2133 anti-tank and 2126 anti-personnel mines were laid for every kilometre of the frontage it was defending. In total, nearly 640,000 mines of various types were laid before and during the offensive.

The Red Army exploited every opportunity to harness the terrain. This included the building of steep banks along rivers, the setting up of tree barriers with explosive charges in copses and forests. Bunkers were heavily disguised by vegetation so that their presence was unknown until they opened fire. False bunkers were constructed. Villages whose inhabitants had been evacuated were incorporated into the defensive zones and turned into fortresses with their own nests of anti-tank guns, supporting artillery and troops equipped for tank killing.

The key element in the defensive design was however allocated to the artillery. All of the 31,000 anti-tank guns and all other calibres ranging from 203, 152, 122, 85, 76 and 45mm in barrels and mortars down to 60mm were integrated into the overall plan for anti-tank defence and were so sighted as to provide extremely heavy fire support to the anti-tank strong points. To bring down 'curtain fire' on the enemy and also effect the rapid manoeuvring of artillery pieces to address new targets, a network of fire control points was established with secure communications to the rear. In the event of an enemy breakthrough the crews of heavy 152 and 122mm guns as well as those of the 85mm anti-aircraft guns which were dispersed through the salient in large numbers. The provision of effective AA defences was deemed to be vital, given that it was expected that most Luftwaffe air operations would be in direct support of the panzer formations. The 85mm weapons were distributed among no fewer than nine anti-aircraft artillery divisions, 40 regiments, 17 battalions and five batteries of anti-aircraft artillery fielding additional calibres ranging from 14.5 through to 45 and 76mm. This firepower was augmented by the rocket artillery, both in ground-mounted M-30 frame launchers and lorry-mounted *Katyusha* launchers. 432 of the former and 105 of the latter were allocated to 13th Army while the Voronezh Front was fielding 88 and 7th Guards Army 47. The three-month hiatus in operations permitted the Soviets to assemble vast stocks of shells and rockets both in and behind the front lines, with reinforcement prior to the commencement of the battle taking place at night.

While firmly anchored on the fixed defences, Soviet strategy for containing the German offensive did not rest upon them alone. Integral to the whole plan for blunting the drive of the panzers was the availability of a mass of armour stationed within the salient that could be deployed to contest and seal any breach in the defences on either front. Although Rokossovsky had deployed a tank regiment to serve with 13th Army in the second echelon of the Central Front, its primary tank support lay in the 2nd Tank Army as the reserve echelon. Comprising the 3rd and 16th Tank Corps, to which was attached the 11th Tank Brigade, the Central Front thus disposed of some 1785 tanks at the start of the offensive, providing the Soviets with a definite advantage in numbers over those of Ninth Army. On the Voronezh Front, Vatutin had deployed a number of his tank formations amongst the units of the 6th and 7th Guards Armies. One tank brigade and three tank regiments were deployed in the first echelon of the two formations, with a further three tank brigades and two tank regiments in the second. However, the primary armoured formation was 1st Tank Army comprising two Tank Corps – the 6th, 31st and the 3rd Mechanised Corps – which between them were fielding 625 tanks and self-propelled guns as of 1 July. This formation was deployed to the rear of 6th Guards Army covering the Oboyan/Kursk sector and provided part of the Front reserve forces occupying the third defence line. In total, the 1704 tanks spread throughout the deployment of 6th, 7th Guards Army and 1st Tank Army were not numerically superior to Manstein's powerful armoured formations. Although not intended for employment in the defensive phase of the battle, the reserve armour stationed with the Steppe Reserve could provide a further 1639 machines as of 4 July, should the need arise.

Over the course of the enforced combat hiatus between March and the beginning of July – the longest such during the course of the conflict on the Eastern Front – the participating troops of all arms involved in the defence of the salient were put through a hectic training programme. The crews of the thousands of T-34s, KV-1s, T-70s and other AFVs became the best prepared for any operation yet conducted. The effectiveness of artillery crews were also honed, with training conducted in mass fire exercises many miles behind the front-lines. So too with the infantry, in order to combat the oft-seen 'tank-flight' – the panic which had so characterised the reaction of the Red Army soldier when confronted by masses of German armour.

In parallel to the defensive preparations, was the ongoing quest to secure intelligence information. In the three month period prior to the launch of *Zitadelle*, numerous deep ranging Soviet reconnaissance teams penetrated the German lines or parachuted behind them to secure information on the identity, make-up and disposition of the assembling enemy forces. Many brought back German prisoners for interrogation. Others worked in tandem with the partisans, who were allocated the same role, as well as being tasked with the destruction of German railway traffic and the ambushing of road convoys, one of the priority targets being those transporting POL (Petrol, Oil and Lubricants) supplies to the front. This activity was to rise to a crescendo prior to the offensive. The use of radio direction finding teams allowed the Soviets to build a fair picture of the assembling German formations – especially in the South. The Soviet Air Force flew many long-range reconnaissance sorties that enabled them to build a detailed picture of the growing German preparations.

The sophistication of Soviet preparations was not just confined to materiel. Indeed, it could be argued that it was the *maskirovka* (deception) measures adopted by the Red Army designed to engender in the enemy mind a false impression not just of the strength of the defences, but more importantly, of what the actual Soviet strategy underpinning the whole of their operation was, that played such a major role in defeating *Zitadelle*.

From the very start of their preparations, it was assumed that the Germans would reconnoitre the salient on a daily basis, and that this German aerial activity could not be prevented. Herein lay the

'CONCEAL, CREATE, CONFUSE'

'Did the enemy know about the organisation of a firm defence in the rear of our fronts? He knew. And that played a positive role. The enemy thought that were preparing *only* [author italics] for a defensive battle. As the enemy prepared, we prepared. The main thing was not to conceal the fact of our preparations, but rather the force and means, the time of our counteroffensive and the nature of our defence. As the enemy prepared, we prepared.'

General I. Konev, Commander of the
Steppe Front

subtlety of the Soviet deception plan – sorties flown on a daily basis were necessary to permit the Germans to see, albeit to a limited degree, what the Red Army was doing. This was deemed to be an essential component to the unfolding Soviet strategy.

In their concern to foster and reinforce this deception, the Soviets deliberately chose on occasions to refrain from attacking enemy tank concentrations belonging to Ninth Army, whose presence close to the front had been observed by aerial reconnaissance. Nothing was to be done to permit the Germans to believe that their offensive intentions had been discovered in case this prompted them to change their plan.

More active *maskirovka* measures included the building of false airfields within the salient (which the Luftwaffe proceeded to bomb) and construction of an immense number of dummy positions. Troop and material reinforcement was conducted by night, as was troop rotation out of the salient, for training many miles behind it. So successful were the Soviets in realising their objectives by these varied deception measures, that when the offensive finally materialised, the Germans had not only underestimated the scale and sophistication of the defence system they were assailing, but also misconstrued the very strategy that underpinned its construction.

The German Tactics

Even though German units had 'photos which covered every square kilometre' in the southern sector of the salient by the time *Zitadelle* began, and while they clearly revealed many genuine Soviet positions, most were so well camouflaged as to be invisible to airborne cameras and the photo interpretation teams. Hence, German planning was based upon a false picture of the scale of the defences, or no picture at all, only to be confirmed once the offensive began as they found themselves enmeshed in a series of seemingly endless series of fortifications and minefields.

Hitler's script for *Zitadelle* required that the panzers be used in a fashion that was the antithesis of how those in the *Panzerwaffe* believed Germany's mobile assets should be employed. The question for Manstein and Model was how best to ensure enough operational panzers survived the passage through the defences, so that once they reached open country, the encirclement could be successfully concluded.

Manstein decided to employ all his armoured formations from the outset as one massive battering ram. He believed that by hurling thousands of tanks and assault guns of 4th Panzer Army at the enemy, he could force the early breach in their defences the plan required. Model however, chose a different approach. He decided first to employ his infantry divisions supported by just one panzer division and numerous assault gun formations to effect breaches in the enemy defences on the opening day, so that on the following, he could feed in his panzer formations to effect the decisive breakthrough.

Central to both was the role of the Luftwaffe. Although the air force had always functioned primarily as the first echelon in German offensive operations, *Zitadelle* would see this role magnified in importance and at the same time circumscribed. Luftwaffe assets – with 70 per cent of its front line strength committed to this operation – were 'tied' by virtue of the relative weakness of the ground forces to sorties that directly serviced the needs of the troops on the battlefield. They were to be the substitute for the artillery that the *Heer* was lacking.

It was presumed by the Germans that the minefields they would encounter would be massive and the deployments of anti-tank guns in *pakfronts* would be huge. Apart from three specialised *funklenk* units employing Borgward B.IV remote-controlled demolition vehicles allocated to Ninth Army, all other formations in the offensive had to employ *pionere* to lift mines by hand!

Nonetheless, the German believed that the key to unlocking the Soviet defences would be by attacks from closely co-ordinated all arms teams deployed in the *panzerkeil* – the tank wedge – and given extremely close support by the Luftwaffe. Employment of Tigers and Ferdinands at the *schwerpunkt* with their strong armour and heavy firepower could impart the momentum. These machines were seen as providing 'bait' for the *pakfronts* which would permit the medium panzers and SPWs with their infantry then to execute their part of the assault plan. The attachment of SPGs would allow medium and heavy artillery to be deployed far quicker to bring supporting fire down on difficult positions.

In the months before the battle German units undertook much training on mocked up enemy positions. The Ferdinands of the 654th PanzerJäger Regiment undertook their training on mock Soviet positions outside of Rouen in northern France before transfer to the East.

HIDDEN MINES

For the panzer divisions in the south of the salient the experience of encountering minefields – many of which had been laid months before and were disguised by grass or crops – was summed up by one German tank commander after the battle: 'Neither minefields nor pakfronts could be detected until the first tank blew up, or the Russian anti-tank guns opened fire.'

The Days Before Battle

One major structural weakness in the German order of battle and of which senior commanders were profoundly aware even before *Zitadelle* began was the dearth of infantry divisions available to support the panzers. In a combat environment more akin to fighting in built up areas, which experience had long shown rendered tanks highly vulnerable unless provided with adequate infantry support, there were none to spare other than those allocated. Manstein tried on many occasions to acquire more infantry divisions but only one was available, and as it was, the 167th Infantry Division would not be in place to execute its allotted role until after the offensive began, as it was first tasked with supporting 11th Panzer Division.

As high summer beckoned on the steppe, as June moved into July, the Red Army had already been stood up and stood down on no fewer than three occasions as Stavka had responded to warnings supplied to it by 'Lucy' concerning the imminence of the German offensive. Finally, on the night of 2 July, Vatutin and Rokossovsky in addition to the commanders of the Western, Bryansk, South-western and Southern Fronts were informed that the enemy would go over to the offensive no later than four days hence. Although this intelligence was derived mainly from 'Lucy' following Hitler's final conference with his commanders the day before, Zhukov was to observe that despite the enemy's attempts at limited diversionary operations, the sheer scale of the forward movement of his offensive assets into their assembly positions confirmed the warning.

Throughout the salient, Soviet troops had been ordered to expect a major German assault and placed on heightened alert with the injunction that nothing be done to suggest to the enemy that his intentions had been divined. To that end, observation posts were constantly manned by officers and troopers were forbidden to move any farther than 100 metres from their trenches. All radios were now tuned in to specific pre-determined frequencies with only essential messages being despatched and in coded, ten-second bursts. Now, at last, the time had finally come to see whether the three months of intensive preparations and training which had seen the expertise of the Red Army soldiery raised to an unprecedented

BATTERING RAM

'The main purpose of the Ferdinand is to batter its way through a well fortified established front and open the way for the following tank units.'
Heinz Guderian, Inspector General of Panzer Troops

level of effectiveness would be enough to face down the still extremely potent German forces.

Access to the decisions taken in Hitler's highest circle via 'Lucy' was indeed remarkable as within 24 hours of his meeting at Rastenburg with the highest ranking officers participating in the offensive, the substance of his speech had been communicated to the Kremlin. 'I have decided to fix the starting date of *Zitadelle* for the fifth of July' – just four days away. After months of delays the German leader had committed the Wehrmacht to its greatest offensive in the East since *Barbarossa*. In offering up an explanation for the many delays, it was his focus on Italy that revealed where his true concerns lay. He stated that as long as there remained the possibility of an Allied landing in Italy he had needed to hold the offensive in abeyance. Now that he felt assured, at least in the short term, that such a landing would not occur, he felt able to proceed in Russia, confident that *Zitadelle* would be successfully concluded in time to permit forces from the East to be transferred to the west to deal with such a contingency.

Nonetheless, his more perceptive listeners must surely have inferred from his comments Hitler's likely response if his intelligence prediction was in error and the Allies carried out their expected landing even while *Zitadelle* was in progress, for the German leader had indicated where his immediate priority lay, and even at this late date, it was not in Russia! In closing, he also stressed the limited nature of the enterprise. It was above all about disrupting Red Army intentions for the rest of the summer; in short, to provide the German Army with 'a breathing space'. While the prestige of victory and great plunder was eminently desirable, time was the greater prize: time in which to re-deploy forces from an Eastern Front rendered temporarily quiescent by victory at Kursk to defeat the expected landings in Europe before the end of 1943. Thereafter, Hitler believed, he could once more turn his attention to Russia.

As the Soviet troops in the salient stood to, German forces had already begun to move into their jumping off positions for the start of the offensive. Forward movement had started on the night of 29 June. By nightfall on 3 July, the bulk of the attacking formations were in place on either flank of the salient and dispersed under cover, with the massive exercise apparently successful in its objective of not arousing the suspicion of the Soviets. It was not until the following day that many of the units of *Luftflotten* 4 and 6 flew into their forward operating bases around Orel and Kharkov.

Dawn on 4 July brought an eerie silence that lasted the better part of the day. Except for a late afternoon pre-offensive attack by the *Grossdeutschland* division on the left of 4th Panzer Army's line – to secure the low hills immediately to the fore – and which lasted through to the evening, even the desultory small arms fire and occasional tank gun and artillery salvoes that had punctuated the daily round on the various sectors of the front throughout the previous months ceased. Only the rumble of persistent thunder and the patter of heavy rain disturbed the tranquillity.

The calm was however illusory; hidden amidst the rural vista lay immense forces. Concentrated on either neck of the salient amongst the numerous copses that dotted the landscape, dispersed among the orchards of the state farms and deployed along the snaking lines of *balkas* screened by camouflage netting were dispersed German and Soviet tanks by the thousand. Spread across this immense frontage were over 1.5 million men decked out in field grey and olive green, steeling themselves for the coming trial of arms. After months of intense preparation, these two huge lavishly equipped forces were as springs compressed to their maximum, awaiting the signal to release their pent-up energies and hurl themselves upon one another. The issue of five days of cold rations and one of schnapps accompanied by a final message from the Führer exhorting his troops onto victory finally signalled that the months of waiting were over.

F.W. Mellenthin (later Major-General) who was serving as Chief of Staff of 48th Panzer Corps, was later to observe that the morale of the German troops 'was of the highest; they were prepared to endure any losses and carry out any task given to them' (an observation that would have equally applied to their Soviet counterparts). Nevertheless, his rider was bitter: 'Unhappily they had been set the wrong tasks.' He continued in a vein that eloquently captured the tale of strategic mismanagement that governed this whole operation:

> Instead of seeking to create the conditions in which manoeuvre would be possible by strategic withdrawals or surprise attacks in quiet sectors, the German Supreme Command could think of nothing better than to fling our magnificent panzer divisions against Kursk, which had now become the strongest fortress in the world.

THE GERMAN OFFENSIVE

5 July: Zitadelle Begins

4th Panzer Army

For the Germans, awaiting the beginning of the offensive, tension was raised at 2230 hours (Berlin time) a hurricane of fire descended upon the assembly positions of 4th Panzer Army and Army Detachment Kempf, followed four hours later on Ninth Army's positions. On both faces of the salient, this long planned for 'disruption barrage' by massed Soviet artillery ranged across the enemy lines and then fell silent.

The delay to the German timetable was minimal and at 0410 hours along the frontage of 4th Panzer Army, hundreds of heavy and medium artillery pieces together with massed *werfer* batteries opened up on the Soviet lines. On cue, the Luftwaffe then appeared overhead to deliver their contribution. The bombers had been scrambled early as radar had detected an incoming Soviet raid targeted at the numerous airfields around Kharkov. These were, at that point, crowded with bomber and fighter units. As warning flares snaked into the sky, the bombers cleared the bases and fighters headed towards the incoming Soviet aircraft. The subsequent air battle was to figure as one of the largest of the war up to that time and saw the Luftwaffe win this opening round.

Used constantly throughout the offensive, the Stuka was very much the Wehrmacht's flying artillery. However, many were lost and Kursk was its swan song as a dive bomber.

The South of the Salient

Deployed from left to right along 4th Panzer Army's frontage was the 3rd Panzer, 48th Panzer Corps and 11th Panzer Division and the II SS Panzer Corps. At 0500, Hoth's armoured fist of 1149 panzers, StuGs and SPGs began their assault on the Soviet defences. For the Panthers attacking on the left of the village of Butovo, matters went awry when over 30 bogged down in marshy terrain. The remainder were pulled back and attached to *Grossdeutschland*'s panzer regiment, which, thrusting forward to the right of the village, struck out towards its first objective – the heavily fortified settlement of Cherkasskoye. By 0900 *Grossdeutschland* and 11th Panzer Division

The German Offensive

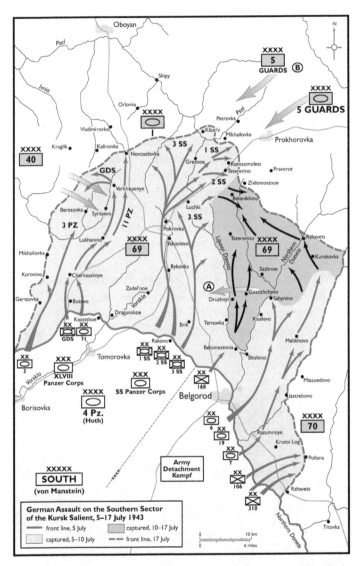

The massive armoured fist that comprised 4th Panzer Army that was launched against the defences of the Red Army's Voronezh Front on 5 July was one of the most powerful assemblages of tanks and assault guns the German Army ever deployed for one operation.

had fought its way through very heavy defences to the lower slope on which the village was located.

The fighting for Gertsovka, which was under assault by 3rd Panzer and at Cherkasskoye, was ferocious. The Germans had no choice but to confront the defenders head on, employing the same tactics being employed by all other German tank formations in dealing with the enemy defences. Once the well camouflaged bunkers and *pakfronts* revealed themselves by their own fire, they were targeted by the Tigers, other panzers and assault guns. Even though supported by continual attacks by Stukas flying in relays, it took until early afternoon for 11th Panzer Division to breach the defences on the eastern flank of Cherkasskoye aided by *FlammPanzer* IIIs. At Gertsovka, even reinforcement by two anti-tank gun regiments was not enough to prevent the village from falling to 3rd Panzer Division.

With both villages, which were linchpins in the Soviet first-defence line, having fallen, General Chistyakov, the commander of 6th Guards Army, ordered the survivors to fall back on the second defence line. Although lacking Tigers, 3rd Panzer and the 332nd Infantry Division

Panthers line up before the beginning of the offensive. They had arrived just days before the start and a number were lost immediately due to engine fires.

The Luftwaffe deployed Hs129s equipped with underbelly 30mm cannon at Kursk. They proved to be effective tank killers.

made headway and advanced five kilometres into the enemy's defensive field by day's end. The fall of Korovino before nightfall saw the capture of the western anchor point of the Soviet first defence line.

By 0900, the three SS divisions had penetrated the first defensive line even though Chistyakov had overseen a massive strengthening of defences along the expected line of advance of SS Panzer Corps. The mile-deep first defence line was manned by the veteran 52nd Grenadier Division and the 375th Division. It was thus with more than a degree of incredulity that he had to contend with a decisive breakthrough of his first defence line within hours of the opening of the German offensive. In this the SS Panzer Corps had been aided by close air support provided by Henschel Hs-129s and Fw-190s of the *Schlachtfleiger* dropping SD-1 and 2 'cluster bombs'

At the outset the SS Panzer Corps found itself advancing into huge fields of ripe wheat and grass, many of which had been sown with mines.

amongst the Soviet defences and reaching infantry even in deeply dug trenches.

The corps had been drawn up on a narrow frontage of 12 kilo-metres in a huge *panzerkeil* with the two Tiger companies of *Leibstandarte Adolf Hitler* and *Das Reich* at the point. To their rear, were the medium panzers and StuGs followed by the *grenadiere* and *pionere* in SPWs, and the mobile artillery of *Wespes, Grilles* and *Hummels. Totenkopf* was echeloned to their right and tasked with protecting their flank from attack but only until such time as III Panzer Corps drew up alongside the advancing SS formation.

The SS advance began without difficulty. Moving along corridors through minefields cleared during the night and deploying into their attack formations, the Soviets responded by opening up with their pre-ranged artillery. To this was added machine gun, anti-tank gun and anti-tank rifle fire as the hidden positions exposed themselves. The panzers set about reducing bunkers as infantry began to clear the trenches. Combat with the defenders became a very bloody affair as spades and bayonets became the weapons of choice. Although the SS assault was proceeding in a systematic fashion, it was becoming clear that the opposition and defences being encountered were unprecedented. Nonetheless, four hours after the assault had begun the SS divisions had breached the mile-deep defence line across the breath of their frontage. Five fortified villages in the first defence line had been stormed and the panzers were now deploying to drive on the second.

Although the Germans had faced a small number of tanks amidst the first defence line, it was only when they began to advance on the second that the first heavy tank engagements ensued. T-34s and T-70s from units of 1st Tank Army had been sent forward by Katukov to slow the SS advance. This abridged account illustrates the impact these tanks made wherever they were engaged:

> We see two T-34s stationed on the heights to the north. The first shells land near us … We move forward to take up a better firing position (German tanks preferred to fire from the halt). Load, unlock, shoot! A hit! We pursue. The first T-34 is burning. Our neighbour has destroyed the second. About forty enemy tanks appear on the horizon. They advance past the blazing wrecks of the first two, then stop, shoot, then move forward again, this time firing on the move, one shell after another … we open fire on the T-34s. The tank battle has really begun in earnest. The two sides face each other on slopes 1000 metres apart. Both sides

want to sway fate with their shooting. All of the Tigers are firing now. The fighting rises to a climax, but the men who operate these machines must remain calm. They aim quickly and respond to orders quickly. We move forward a few metres; move to the right then to the left, manoeuvring outside of the enemy's sights. He however comes into the cross hairs of our own and we fire. We count the blazing torches of enemy tanks … After one hour twelve T-34s are ablaze. The remaining thirty are circling back and forth and firing off their shells in a bid to hit us. The battle has lasted for four hours.

The advance of *Das Reich* ground to a halt mid-afternoon when they encountered vast minefields screening the Russian second line. Some kilometres to the west *Leibstandarte Adolf Hitler* made better progress. By mid-afternoon it had captured the village of Bykova. Marshal Zhukov: 'In the afternoon, the enemy began a second advance with heavy Tiger tanks. This time he succeeded in breaking the resistance of the 52nd Guards Rifle Division.'

As the most heavily armoured and armed of the panzers, the Tigers were almost always employed at the front of the advancing German tank columns.

The optimism generated by the seeming rapidity of the advance now prompted HQ to issue the order that the second Soviet defence line was to be penetrated and the river Psel reached by day's end. The Soviets were to rapidly disabuse German expectations when the leading elements of *Leibstandarte* ran into minefields, pakfronts and fortifications near the village of Yakovlevo. No further advance was registered for the rest of the day.

On the right, *Totenkopf* had ground through the defences of the 52nd Army and was engaged in a series of fights with enemy armour. By late afternoon, with the Tiger Co in the lead, the division had broken the enemy resistance covering the second defence line, and having captured the fortified village of Yakhontovo, had then broken through it. Minefields however rendered eleven Tigers unserviceable by days end. All were returned to combat in the days ahead.

Darkness found all three divisions firmly ensconced 20 kilometres into the defensive field of Sixth Guards Army with *Leibstandarte* positioned to drive through the remaining Soviet defences on the morrow. It was on the 5th that the SS divisions incurred their highest losses in the battle. Strength returns recorded that 4th Panzer Army had 953 operational tanks and assault guns available for service on the morrow. Optimism was however tempered by the problems attending Army Detachment Kempf. Indeed, the delay in this formation's advance would begin to act as a drag in its turn on that of the SS Panzer Corps in the days ahead, as *Totenkopf* was hived off to act as flank guard in lieu of III Panzer Corps, which had been designated with that task in the planning.

Army Detachment Kempf

The problems on this sector began at the outset. Not only had the one bridgehead that the Germans had on the east bank of the Donets, packed with eight infantry battalions, come in for heavy attention from Soviet artillery in the early hours, but come dawn, the vital 24-ton tank bridge being thrown across the river was as yet incomplete. Its fate was recorded by Clemens Graf Kageneck, the commander of schwere Panzer Abteilung 503:

> I stood on the bank of the Donets in the grey light of dawn on 5 July to watch the crossing of our tanks into the bridgehead. The engineers had worked feverishly during the night and the bridge was 80 per cent completed. Then suddenly, a 'red sunrise' arose on the far side as hundreds of Stalin's organs hurled their rockets exactly onto the crossing site. The bridge was totally demolished and the engineers, unfortunately, suffered heavy losses.

A Panzer IV of the HQ detachment of 7th Panzer Division climbs a muddy bank on the eastern bank of the Donets on the opening day of Zitadelle.

In consequence, elements of 6th Panzer had to move south and use the bridge serving that sector of the front only to find that it could not cross because of the traffic that had already made it to the far bank. 19th Panzer and the 2nd Company of the schwere Panzer Abteilung 503 (which had been split up, its three Tiger companies allocated to one each of the panzer divisions of III Panzer Corps) had found themselves enmeshed in dense Soviet defences with the Tigers blundering into a minefield, resulting in 13 of the 14 heavy tanks being lost at the very outset of the battle. Although not write-offs, it took at least three days before they were all back in service after repair. The 1st Company of 503 fared no better. It had managed to cross the southern bridge but had been stopped outside of the village of Stary Gorod. The upshot for the remnants of 6th Panzer was that they spent the rest of the day moving ever southward in search of a crossing point and did not enter combat at all on 5 July!

A 24-ton bridge had been assembled seven kilometres to the south of Belgorod to permit the medium Mark IIIs and IVs of 7th Panzer Division to get to the far bank but its weight-bearing capacity ruled out Tigers. A much larger 60-ton bridge was under construction but rather than wait for its completion, the decision was taken for the Tigers of 3/503 to ford the river. However, the lead tank grounded on the far bank in marshy ground and the decision was taken to await completion of the bridge. Heavy Soviet artillery fire destroyed the smaller bridge, leaving the forward elements of 7th Panzer isolated on the far bank. Gun and *katyusha* fire now moved on to target the larger bridge which was not destroyed but it was not until midday that it was completed and only then did the Tigers finally cross. They were then confronted with a mass of fire from well layered fortifications. They did what they were doing elsewhere in the salient: bunkers were reduced and nests of 'crash-booms' were cleared permitting the infantry to move into close combat with Soviet troopers. By mid-afternoon, the Tigers had advanced as far as the fortified village of Razumnoye where they found themselves in a running battle with Soviet armour that sortied from a number of copses and collective farms dotted over the rolling plain.

Although the *Stukageschwaden* provided extensive support throughout the course of the 5th and in the days to come, nothing could be done to catch up with the delay that was being imposed on Hoth's critical timetable by the formidable defences Kempf's forces were encountering. Shumilov's 7th Guards Army had turned the whole of the eastern bank of the Donets for some ten miles below Belgorod into an immensely sophisticated killing ground. While by day's end Kempf was confident that he would have the bulk of his forces across the river by early next day, his optimism that the Soviet defences would be penetrated quickly thereafter was misplaced. In the following days III Panzer Corps, which was operating on an extremely critical timetable, struggled to break free. This would affect the advance of the SS Panzer Corps in the days ahead. On the first day of *Zitadelle* the German timetable in the south had clearly gone awry.

Ninth Army

The North of the Salient
Forty minutes after the opening of Ninth Army's barrage waves of Stukas and medium bombers appeared overhead to target the identified elements in the Soviet first defence line. They were flying the first of many sorties that Luftflotte 6 would launch in support of Model's forces on this opening day of the offensive. Unlike in the south where the huge air battle near Kharkov had temporarily 'cleared the sky' for the Luftwaffe, in the north the air operations of the Germans would be heavily contested by enemy fighter squadrons from the outset. The ground forces would find themselves under almost continual assault by the shturmovik and bomber formations of Rudenko's 17th Air Army.

In accord with Model's decision, the initial assault was undertaken primarily by the infantry formations, with six out of his seven panzer divisions held back for later commitment, with only 20th Panzer

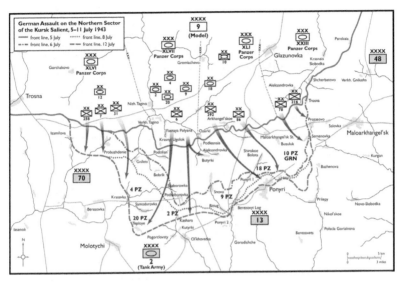

Ninth Army's offensive was launched along a narrow front of 40 kilometres with the main thrust being delivered by Lemelsen's XLVII Panzer Corps. The front line for 12 July illustrates just how little progress the Germans made in the north of the salient.

Division seeing combat on the first day. Alongside, however, and going into action in support of the infantry were six StuG brigades, the Tigers of the first and second companies of schwere Panzer Abteilung 505 and the 90 Ferdinands and 45 *Brummbären* of PanzerJäger Regiment 656. In hindsight, this was seen to be an error that possibly deprived Model of his only opportunity of achieving a breakthrough of the Central Front.

As in the south, first encounters with the Soviet defences revealed how sophisticated, deep and formidable they were. Having made passage through the corridors in the minefields cleared overnight, both infantry and armour found themselves targeted by the full gamut of weaponry deployed by 13th Army.

On the extreme left of Model's frontage the 258th Infantry Division had been tasked with advancing southward and parallel to the Orel-Kursk highway. Its role was to provide flank cover for what was the primary German thrust on the Teploye-Olkhovatka axis. However, the infantry found it impossible to advance any further than the second defensive line in the initial defensive zone because of the sheer weight of enemy fire, even though supported by SPGs and assault guns. So ferociously and effectively did the 280th Rifle Division defend their positions, that the Germans in this sector, even when reinforced with more armour, could make no further headway over the course of the next five days.

Nor was there any real success on the right of the German front, where XXIII Corps was tasked to rapidly seize the town of MaloArchangelsk. Although unable to provide this formation with a panzer division – he could spare none – Freissner's three infantry divisions had been allocated the 78th (Sturm) Division, which while ostensibly an infantry formation, was equipped with 72 StuGs, large numbers of *Nebelwerfers*, a higher allocation of artillery and the temporary attachment of the 45 Ferdinands. It was presumed that the latter, by virtue of their heavy armour and firepower, would impart a massive weight to the German assault and enable Freissner to blast through the three divisions of the 18th Army manning the defences before MaloArchangelsk and screening the approaches to the important fortified village of Ponyri.

As elsewhere, German expectations were confounded by the enemy defences, the weight of fire directed at the infantry and armour and the immense minefields that screened the enemy bunkers and trenches. It was a minefield that now blocked the advance of the Ferdinands in their approach to fortified Hill no: 257.7., the linchpin of the Soviet first defence line. To neutralise this danger, Borgward B.IV explosive carriers of Panzer Corps (Fkl) 314 moved forward under heavy enemy fire to deposit their 500kg charges. These machines were remotely controlled from StuG command vehicles. The attempt to blow a lane through the minefield was impeded by the Soviets laying down a heavy artillery barrage on the field itself resulting in the decision to send forward the Ferdinands, come what may. A number fell victim – their tracks

A Ferdinand heavy assault gun drives forward into the Soviet defence lines.

being blown off – but enough got through to help seize the hill after very fierce fighting.

Matters were unfolding more successfully in the centre of Ninth Army's line, in the six-mile sector between Wech-Tagino through to the Orel-Kursk railway. This is where Model had both concentrated and unleashed his *schwerpunkt* in his bid to capture the key settlements of Teploye and Olkhovatka. Following the barrage and air strikes, the 6th, 86th and 292nd Infantry Divisions with heavy assault gun and other SPG support moved forward to engage the first defensive line and as with all other German formations, ran straight into a wall of fire from all calibres and extensive minefields. Nonetheless, by 0800, the penetration of the defences of the 15th Division by 6th Infantry Division was sufficiently promising for the two companies of schwere Panzer Abteilung 505 to be ordered forward. Although the 3rd company was still en-route from Germany, the 26 Tigers that advanced into the Russian lines represented the largest concentration of these heavy panzers committed on the first day of *Zitadelle*. Attached to 505 was the 2nd Company of Funklenk 312.

The Germans empoyed many Panzerjager – lightly armoured, tracked anti-tank guns.

Many StuGs and panzers on both necks of the salient were put out action by mines.

The German Offensive

The three command StuGs and twelve Borgward demolition vehicles were deployed in front of the Tigers to breach minefields as they advanced. 505 had been tasked to exploit a weakness in the enemy line revealed by prisoner interrogation. Passing through the forward German positions at Novy Chutor, the Tigers crossed the shallow river Oka and advanced southward towards the settlements of Podolyan and Butyrki and into the exposed flank of the 676th Rifle Regiment. Driving forward towards the village of Yasnaya Polyana across fields of yellow rye, there now developed a tank battle that lasted through to midday in which the Soviets threw large numbers of T-34s against the oncoming panzers in a bid to halt their advance. When finally the Tigers secured the village of Butyrki, 42 burning Russian tanks marked their passage. In the wake of the Tigers came the Mark IIIs and IVs of 20th Panzer and by midday, they had secured the village of Podoljan. Success had also attended the Ferdinands and the attached Funklenk company who were operating in support of 86th and 292nd Infantry Divisions. Although they encountered minefields and heavy resistance, they too had secured their immediate objective and had captured the village of Alexsandrovka and linked up with German troops in Butyrki. It has been argued that had more panzer divisions been available for immediate deployment on the 5th, then their commitment here might have provided Model with the breakthrough he was seeking.

By late afternoon, Model's maps were registering an inroad into 13th Army's defensive field of some 3 miles, albeit along a narrow frontage of just four miles. However, and in what was to become a recurring experience in the days ahead, many Soviet troops that had been bypassed in the advance, had not surrendered and gone to ground, popping up again to resume fighting. To secure some degree of rear security, armour had to be sent back from the front line to deal with this nagging problem.

For Rokossovsky, this German thrust now prompted a change in plans. The three Tank Corps of Rodin's 2nd Tank Army were now given new orders to shift from their initial area of deployment to

These 203mm howitzers were the heaviest calibre gun fielded by the Red Army.

The 76.2mm 'crash-boom' seen here and the 45mm gun were the most common anti-tank gun encountered by the Germans at Kursk.

A Panther and wounded German soldiers from GD division, 48th Panzer Corps, take a breather on the steppe.

the south of Ponyri to the north so as to screen the approaches to Teploye, Olkhovatka and also Ponyri. In effect they were to take up a position so as to block the primary German thrust, which had clearly revealed itself as coming to the west of the Orel-Kursk railway line and not the east as he had originally assumed. This was no small task as Rodin had to move 600 tanks, 500–600 guns and mortars and nearly 50,000 men so that they would be in place ensconced in the second defence line by dawn the following day. Rokossovsky also fed in more divisions to MaloArchangelsk and the rear of 2nd Tank Army. He had little doubt that 6 July would see an all-out effort by Model to effect the breach of the Soviet defences in order to capture Ponyri and thereafter thrust south-east to Olkhovatka, in an effort to outflank the Soviet defensive system on the heights.

6–11 July: 4th Panzer Army

4th Panzer Army's resumed its advance at first light with Soviet artillery laying down huge bombardments on the leading German formations. The next four days would not witness the success of the first day of the offensive –it would be a long, slow and bloody grind with frequent, heavy tank battles as Vatutin's forces fought desperately to prevent 4th Panzer Army, as the Russians thought was their aim, from penetrating the entirety of their second defensive zone and crossing the river Psel. The Soviets had to prevent this at all costs, as breaking out into the open country beyond the river with its promise of freedom of manoeuvre was the key to the enemy design to destroy the salient.

The reported increase in Soviet resistance fed back to 48th Panzer Corps and II SS Panzer Corps headquarters was a direct consequence of Vatutin's order to feed Kutukov's 1st Tank Army into the line and dispose its resources along a front from the village of Melovoe, eastward through to Syrtsevo. This massive infusion of might, constituting 525 T-34s, 109 T-70s, SPGs and all the other armament resources that now constituted the complement of a Tank Army, deployed alongside the forces of 6th Army. In addition, Vatutin moved other tank formations into new positions – the consequence of which was to raise the total of tanks fed in to line by a further 400-plus machines. Overnight, the Soviets had raised the number of tanks available to confront the advance of 4th Panzer Army by a thousand machines.

Numbers notwithstanding, the encounter with Tigers, Panthers and assault guns and even PanzerJäger, all mounting armament that could penetrate the frontal armour of the T-34 at some range, had caused a rapid re-appraisal of how the tank formations could be best used. The decision – by the people on the spot – namely Vatutin, Vasilevsky (Stavka representative) and Khruschev (front commissar) was to have approximately half of these tanks 'dug in' so that only the turrets could be seen. They would thereby

The Wespe *SPG mounted a 105mm howitzer on a converted Panzer II chassis. It first saw service at Kursk.*

strengthen the anti-tank defence in the second fortified zone. The other half were to remain mobile in tank formations allocated to serve on the flanks of the advancing Germans. The latter decision would soon prove to have been astute, as the near constant assaults on the flanks of both the 48th Panzer Corps and the II SS Panzer Corps in the days ahead was to prove to be one of the major factors contributing to the ultimate failure of the German assault in the south of the salient.

As the core element of 48th Panzer Corps, the *Grossdeutschland* division was engaged in extremely heavy fighting throughout the day as it encountered very dense Soviet defences and was under constant heavy bombardments as it attempted to advance northward. The divisional history:

Operation Zitadelle 1943

A heavy tank battle developed in the broad cornfields and flat terrain there against the Bolsheviks grimly defending their second line of resistance. Earth bunkers, deep positions with built-in flame throwers and especially well dug-in T-34s, excellently camouflaged, made the advance extremely difficult.

By day's end on 6 July, *Grossdeutschland* was still enmeshed in the second defensive zone. Tank losses had increased to 134 – especially from mines, as the panzers blundered into fields, leading to correspondingly high losses amongst troops sent in to recover them. To maintain the weight of the offensive, it was vital to have every tank retrieved, repaired and returned to service as soon as possible assuming the damage was not extensive. Only at Luchanino was *Grossdeutschland* able to achieve a major success. The experience was much the same for 11th and 3rd Panzer as they tried to press through the defensive field, the former having taken the village of Olkhovka in tandem with 167th Infantry Division. 3rd Panzer had

Tigers of Das Reich *prepare to continue their advance into the enemy defence positions. By 12 July* Das Reich *would have no serviceable Tigers available.*

An SPW advances across the steppe while in the distance a tank blows up, generating a huge plume of smoke. This was a common sight on the Kursk battlefield.

reached the Pena by dusk, but was still some distance from the river Psel, which it will be recalled had been the Corps objective for the end of the 6th.

Once again, the SS divisions made the running, albeit against ferocious opposition. As *Leibstandarte Adolf Hitler* and *Das Reich* advanced they found themselves engaged in heavy running battles with Soviet armour that continued through to the late evening. Those Soviet mobile units that had not been dug in, sortied out from their defensive positions to contest the advance. As on the previous day, the T-34s, KV-Is and M-3s suffered heavy losses owing to the range of the German guns. Even so, the SS divisions reported 110 AFVs having 'fallen out' during the course of the day. The measure of the scale of the fighting on the 6th was that it marked the highest AFV losses in 4th Panzer Army for the whole offensive.

Nonetheless, the progress of the two SS divisions and the unprecedented mass of armour they were fielding had generated unexpected gains and was generating great anxiety at the HQ of the Voronezh Front. Having reported to Stalin, Vatutin requested reinforcements and was supported in this matter by Vasilevsky. The latter told 'the boss' that the Voronezh Front's ability to 'conduct further active operations' was now contingent upon receipt of substantial reinforcement. Although earmarked ostensibly for post-Kursk counteroffensive operations, such was the perceived seriousness of the situation that Stalin ordered that 5th Guards Tank Army – the core offensive formation of the Steppe Reserve – now be put at the disposal of Vatutin. The much earlier than anticipated commitment of this huge formation is indicative of just how dangerous the continuing German advance was viewed. Unless such reinforcement was made available, then a breakthrough of the Soviet position to the south of the Psel was viewed as a real possibility.

General Ivan Konev was not at all happy on receipt of the order to release 5th Guards Tank Army but was ordered by Stalin to

Massive reinforcement and relocation of forces by the Soviets took place throughout the battle on both faces of the salient. The biggest was the despatch of 5th Guards Tank Army to assist Vatutin.

comply. Some hours later he met the commander of the formation and ordered him to get his huge force rolling towards the Kursk battlefield. It would take General Rotmistrov's command the best part of a week to traverse the distance. It was Zhukov and Vasilevsky's intention that 5th Guards Tank Army would arrive in the vicinity of the small town of Prokhorovka in time to employ its 600-plus tanks, supporting artillery and infantry to prevent a decisive breakthrough by the SS Panzer Corps and 48th Panzer Corps in their bid to capture Oboyan. Further reinforcement for Vatutin came in the form of the 2nd and 10th Tank Corps, both of which were destined to play major roles in the days ahead.

7 July

The onset of cooler weather and rain was to cause problems for the Germans and aid the Soviets in the days ahead. Rain and mud notwithstanding, Hoth's formations, still numbering over 600 machines, resumed their offense at 0400 on the 7th and were hammering away at the Soviet line the full 30 miles of Chistyakov's frontage from Syrtsevo in the west through to Luchki 1 in the east. Early in the day 48th Panzer Corps finally managed to break out of the enemy defences and into open country. Their progress however was punctuated by numerous, very heavy artillery barrages. Large calibre explosive shells were well able to puncture the thinner hull and turret armour if a panzer was unlucky enough to be hit (more than a few panzers on either neck of the salient were 'written off' in this way). Shortly after dawn, the village of Dubrova had been stormed by elements of *Grossdeutschland* and in concert with 11th Panzer the two formations advanced northwards with the intention of capturing the vital centre of Syrtsevo – the last major fortified position in the second defence line before Oboyan.

The German advance prompted a major response with Katukov unleashing over 100 T-34s of his 3rd Mechanised and 6th Tank Corps with heavy air support to assail the spearheads of *Grossdeutschland*,

Seemingly inexhaustible numbers of T-34s launch yet another attack against the oncoming Germans.

11th Panzer and *Leibstandarte*. The resulting large tank battle lasted many hours. Unlike the previous two days, when Luftwaffe support had been continual, the detachment of elements of Luftflotte 4 northward to aid Ninth Army's efforts found the panzers having to contend with many aerial assaults from IL-2s and medium bombers. Nonetheless, the superior armament and gunnery of the German tanks told as the *Leibstandarte* reported that it had destroyed a least 20 T-34s. As the Soviets fell back in some disorder on the settlements of Syrtsevo and Gremuchi under heavy artillery fire, 48th Panzer Corps resumed its advance in a bid to capture Syrtsevo, only for the Panther regiment to drive into a minefield. Three days after the start of the offensive, just 40 out of 184 of the new panzers were still operational. Although a number had become total losses, by far the largest number had succumbed to breakdowns and mine damage and the bulk were returned to service in subsequent days.

Once more, the thousands of mines and large numbers of 'crash-booms' brought the advance to a halt before Syrtsevo, with the bulk

The German Offensive

of *Grossdeutschland* tied down for the rest of the day. Hill 230, lying to the east of the village was, however, taken. It was not just the Panthers that were falling out. The last of *Grossdeutschland*'s Tigers broke down and by day's end all were under repair. Under covering fire, *Grossdeutschland*'s *pionere* ventured into the minefields to clear paths so that the tanks could advance against the village the following day. Darkness brought little respite for either side. German and Soviet tank crews alike, exhausted by the day's exertions, flopped down beside or underneath their machines and sought to gain some desperately needed rest even as the cacophony of battle continued into the night.

By day's end, Vatutin was facing a difficult situation. Even as 48th Panzer Corps was pushing forward to the immediate south of Oboyan, the SS Panzer Corps had successfully breached his defences some kilometres to the east, thrusting even further northward. Fighting on this axis had been ferocious. Hoth's orders to Hausser for the following day had once more reiterated that Prokhorovka was still his immediate objective and given its proximity to the most forward of the SS units, he hoped that it could be secured by day's end.

The SS advance had resumed in cold mist and by 0545 hours the momentum of the German assault had begun to build as Hausser's forces deployed across the rolling steppe in the lee of heavy Stuka assaults on the Soviet defences. Blocking the path of the SS divisions between Greznoye and Teterevino, lay the remnants of the 52nd and 67th Guards Rifle Divisions. A number of prolonged and fluid tank battles broke out, which lasted intermittently throughout the day. Elements of 1st Tank Army confronted elements of *Leibstandarte* in Luchki 2 and the panzer regiments of the *Leibstandarte* and *Das Reich* around Teterevino. In order to relieve the forward pressure on 6th Guards and 1st Tank Army, Vatutin had ordered attacks by 2nd Guards Tank Corps which had sortied against units of *Totenkopf* still defending the eastern flank of the Panzer Corps. A Soviet account described the effects of the day's combat:

Operation Zitadelle 1943

[T]he enemy had broken through our second defensive position along the line dividing 1st TA and 5th GAC (between Greznoye and Luchki 1). Our army now faced not only to the south but also to the east. This made its front lines ten kilometres longer than before. Our troop strength, however, had dwindled considerably.

A message, intercepted by the Germans, sent by Vatutin stated that on no account must the enemy break through to the Psel. Everything must be done to hold the German assault to the south of the river until the massive reinforcement by 5th Guards Tank Army – but that was, at the earliest, still five days away!

The savagery of the fighting at Ponyri left a number of German panzers destroyed and abandoned.

8 July

Although by the end of the day returns would indicate that 4th Panzer Army had lost a further 125 tanks, those inflicted on the Soviets were much higher, some 300 being claimed by the two Panzer Corps. Such figures give an indication of the intensity of the fighting during the course of the 8th, as 4th Panzer Army continued its drive on Oboyan.

Shortly after 0500, units of *Leibstandarte* and *Das Reich* struck out for the villages of Bol Majatschki and Wesselyi to the north-west, prompting a series of heavy Soviet ripostes between 0900 and midday by waves of T-34s. These rolling tank battles saw the panzer formations and their attendant PaKs forced to rapidly regroup and frequently change direction to counter these Soviet assaults. Although launched with great verve, the T-34s succumbed to the heavier armament of the German panzers such that by midday the SS panzers were stationed either side of Wesselyi. Heavy Soviet attacks persisted throughout the afternoon with one of the strongest launched in the early evening amidst rainstorms and lasting though to dusk. By day's end *Leibstandarte* had driven a wedge in the direction of Solotino, thus forcing apart the 31st Tank Corps and 3rd Mechanised Corps.

To the west, 48th Panzer Corps was involved throughout most of the day in heavy fighting for the settlement of Syrtsevo. Soviet resistance was extremely fierce as the village was a key position in the second defence line. An attempt by 3rd Panzer and *Grossdeutschland* to take the place by storm was thwarted, but a planned counterattack on the extending German left flank by tank units of Moskalenko's mainly uncommitted 38th and 40th Armies had to be aborted as Stalin passed on word that under no circumstances were the Germans to break-through to Oboyan. In consequence, Vatutin had no recourse but to employ Moskalenko's units to reinforce and pack the Soviet defences in the remaining kilometres before the Psel. The latter had to part with one tank

A knocked out Ferdinand.

corps, the majority of his 13 rifle divisions and their organic artillery formations. Although these would take 24 hours to cover the distance and deploy, they would do much to reinforce 6th Guards Army covering the approaches to the Psel bridges.

In the meantime, the defenders of Syrtsevo were exhorted to hold out at all costs. It was only in the mid-afternoon that the Germans were finally able to take the village. Some 30 T-34s had sortied forth only to run into the guns of a *kampfgruppe* from *Grossdeutschland* containing eight Tigers, these having been returned to service overnight. The survivors fled into the village and continued to fight until the place fell. Even then, the German forces found themselves coming under increasingly heavy tank and artillery fire from the far bank of the Pena. This was but a foretaste of the continual threat to 48th Panzer Corps' western flank that would increase greatly in the following days and which would ultimately so tie up the armoured resources of 3rd Panzer and *Grossdeutschland* as to help stop the German advance on the Psel.

In the short term however, the situation had become critical for the Russians as *Grossdeutschland* had begun an immediate redeployment prior to resuming the advance on the next vital town – Verkhopenye. Just a few kilometres to the north-east, 11th Panzer with the SS divisions on its right, had broken through the defences before and had then crossed the main Belgorod–Kursk highway.

SPEARHEAD

'We saw in the distance a large number of tanks. It was impossible to distinguish damaged tanks from those undamaged. The
row began moving. Only a burned field a few hundred metres
wide, nothing else separated us from the enemy. Katukov did
not take the field glasses from his eyes. He mumbled: "They are
re-grouping ... advancing as a spearhead ... I think we
have had it!"'

By late afternoon, the leading elements of the *Grossdeutschland*
panzer regiment had crossed a bridge hastily thrown across the
Pena so that by early evening the town – which was spread out
about a kilometre along on either side of the river bank – was
under heavy attack as more of *Grossdeutschland*'s forces turned
up. The tempo of combat escalated as T-34s came out of the
settlement to attack the panzers, whilst the division's infantry tried
to fight their way in, in the face of large numbers of bunkers, mines
and other defensive impedimenta, all the while under accurate
and heavy artillery fire from the far bank. At dusk, the bulk of the
division was deployed in a tight defensive ring around the eastern
side and would be under bombardment from the ground and the
air all night.

9, 10 and 11 July

Dawn over the south of the salient revealed a grey sky and rain.
4th Panzer Army's timetable was now three days behind schedule.
Although claiming at least 500 enemy tanks destroyed, strength
returns for dawn on the 9th recorded 599 panzers available,
indicating that some 405 machine had been 'lost'. Few however,
were total losses with the bulk in need of short- or long-term repair.
Despite the deficit, Hoth was confident that he retained sufficient
armour to achieve the breakthrough.

Of greatest concern was the slow progress in the advance of III Panzer Corps, as ever since the 5th it had been unable to fulfil its designated role of providing cover for the SS Panzer Corps' extending eastern flank. In consequence, he had had little choice but to 'hive off' a number of his own valuable mobile units for the task. Whilst *Totenkopf* had perforce to undertake this responsibility for the first few days, the arrival of the 167th Infantry Division had finally released it the previous day, with *Das Reich* having to take up the role thereafter. Albeit engaged farther to the north, *Das Reich* was subjected to continuing heavy assaults from 5th Guards Tank Corps and 2nd Tank Corps directed at Hausser's left flank on the approaches to Prokhorovka. The continuing failure of Breith's III Panzer Corps to close this gap would see *Das Reich* successfully pinned down by the Soviets through to 12 July, which meant it would play a minor role in the great tank battle on that date.

48th Panzer Corps

The assault on Verkhopenye resumed at 0600 hours led by Stuka strikes and armour from the panzer regiment. With aid of the panzers and assault guns the eastern part of the town had been cleared by 0830. But 3rd Panzer, tasked with clearing the west bank and lacking heavy armour, was successfully being held by a strengthening Soviet defence, the upshot of which was to expose the lengthening western flank of *Grossdeutschland*. With the eastern part of the town secured, elements of *Grossdeutschland* operating with 11th Panzer their its left pushed forward to secure the next settlement on the map – Novosselovka. En-route there was very heavy fighting as the Germans attempted to displace Soviet defenders from a succession of 'hills'. The *kampfgruppe* found itself engaged with a large number of Soviet tanks and heavy fighting ensued.

Even as forward German elements contemplated a resumption of their advance, an urgent message from Corps HQ required that *Grossdeutschland* change the direction of its *schwerpunkt* to deal with a growing threat to the exposed flank of the formation.

Hoth and von Knobelsdorff determined that remedial action was urgently needed – hence the order to *Grossdeutschland*'s panzer regiment. Although both men assumed this would be a short term measure, with *Grossdeutschland* returning to its primary task within a day or so, such would be the scale of fighting as the Soviets committed more and more formations to pressure the German flank that *Grossdeutschland* would find itself unable to disengage and resume the advance on the Psel crossings. After the 9th, only the Fusilier Regiment of *Grossdeutschland*, 11th Panzer Division and its attached assault gun brigade would remain to maintain the semblance of an advance on Oboyan. Unbeknownst to them, Novosselovka would mark the northern-most point of 48th Panzer Corps advance during *Zitadelle*. Although 3rd Panzer Division had maintained its advance over the first three days of the offensive, its lack of heavy panzers had told as the Soviets increased their defences and tank numbers.

For the remainder of the 9th and the whole of 10 July, *Grossdeutschland* was engaged in a series of very heavy tank battles to the west of the Pena focusing on ownership of a range of heavily fortified Soviet hill positions. In consequence, the pressure on 3rd Panzer was relieved permitting it to advance once more. In partnership with *Grossdeutschland* they succeeded in encircling the Soviet 112th Tank Brigade. Nonetheless, von Mellenthin noted how exhausted the troops were looking and the reduced tank numbers, with 219 available on the 10th.

In essence, for the remainder of the offensive *Grossdeutschland* would be tied down on the west bank countering continual Soviet assaults and although it would destroy a large number of Soviet tanks, the Red Army was prepared to pay in this 'hard currency' to pin down 49th Panzer Corps and stop its drive on the Psel.

SS Panzer Corps

Resuming their advance at 1000 hours the three SS divisions were fielding 249 panzers and StuGs, which, although 202 down, was deemed sufficient to maintain momentum. With Stukas in close support, the panzers fanned out across the steppe. Heavy tank battles broke out throughout the day. Troops of *Leibstandarte Adolf Hitler* and 11th Panzer met near the village of Solotino just before midday and this was stormed shortly thereafter but not before the bridge there was blown by the defenders. The village now came under heavy artillery bombardment.

During the course of the day, the *Leibstandarte* began to vacate its position on the left wing to *Totenkopf,* which then began its assault on the bunkers, trench lines and dug in armour that made up the last Soviet defensive position before the river Psel. The fighting was extremely heavy, with some of the fiercest surrounding the village of Kotchetovka where the headquarters of 6th Guards Army was located. By the afternoon the village had been stormed and the focus of the fighting moved to Hill 241.6, a heavily fortified ridge that offered a commanding view of the short distance remaining to the river. The Soviets resisted tenaciously and *Totenkopf* was assailed though to the evening by large numbers of T-34s of the 24th Guards Tank Brigade. As darkness fell *Totenkopf* was poised to advance the last few kilometres to the river.

For Vatutin, the situation was tempered by two pieces of favourable news; notwithstanding the ferocity of the German assault, there were unmistakable signs of a major re-deployment of the SS Panzer Corps such that its attack axis was being shifting away from the frontal assault on Oboyan towards the north-east. And the diversion of *Grossdeutschland* to service the defence of its western flank had also provided temporary respite on that sector. Both were welcome signs, as the strength of both 6th Guards Army and 1st Tank Army was diminishing rapidly. Furthermore, travelling both day and night, 6th Guards Tank Army had traversed many hundreds of miles and by day's end on the 9th were moving ever closer to their assembly area around Prokhorovka. Following on behind was Zhadov's 5th Guards Army. It would arrive on the 12th and go into battle on the northern bank of the Psel, straight off the march.

The German Offensive

Soviet intelligence was indeed accurate, for Manstein and Hoth had indeed ordered Hausser to begin the pre-planned re-direction of the whole of his command's offensive axis to the north-east and strike out for and secure Prokhorovka, prior to the arrival there of 6th Guards Tank Army.

Assuming that the *Leibstandarte* would carry out its re-deployment overnight, Hausser issued orders that he expected the division to begin its advance at 0600hrs the following day. Operating on *Leibstandarte*'s left flank would be *Totenkopf*, which had been tasked with crossing and then driving along the north bank of the Psel. To the south of the line Teterovino–Storozhevoe–Jamki would be *Das Reich*, which, although still holding defensive positions, was expected to begin its own push to the south of Prokhorovka. With barely 15 kilometres separating *Leibstandarte* from its objective, Hausser expected to have secured the town by day's end. Overnight rain, a slower than anticipated re-deployment, and the failure of *Totenkopf* to secure Hill 222.6 on the northern bank of the Psel in time, saw the attack jump-off fours later than planned.

The timetable was too optimistic. The attack by *Totenkopf* before the river was met with great ferocity, such that it was not until midday that the SS troops had secured a small bridgehead on the far bank. Although provided with Stuka and artillery support throughout the rest of the day, the forces on the northern bank were under attack all through the night with the deteriorating weather conditions preventing a bridge being thrown across for the panzers. The cost to *Totenkopf* was 430 dead, wounded and missing, the highest one-day total by any German division in the offensive. It would not be until the following day that a bridge was finally thrown across the river and armour could move across.

The *Leibstandarte* had finally begun its move at 1045 albeit lacking some of its combat elements in striking out for Prokhorovka. Vatutin's decision of the previous evening to launch a counter-offensive designed in part to encircle the very forces now attacking him found his units in the process of re-deployment even as the German forces thudded into them. In consequence, *Leibstandarte* and *Das Reich* found the enemy unprepared for their assault. Although under heavy attack by 2nd Tank Corps, by 1300 hours the *Komsomolets* State Farm had been captured and the attack on Hill 241.6 begun. This was captured after three and a half hours' fighting. The German troops dug themselves in for the night.

Only one regiment of *Das Reich* was enabled to engage in limited offensive activity. The panzer regiment and the remaining nine Tigers aiding panzer grenadiers in the attack on Storozhevoe, was engaged in very heavy fighting with 2nd Tank Corps, which only gave ground slowly. The remaining strength of *Das Reich* was still engaged a little to the south covering the flank of the other two divisions as they pushed to the north-east and would have to remain so until III Panzer Corps arrived on the scene. But as daylight faded and the Soviets maintained their pressure, this formation was nowhere to be seen, with the implication that the bulk of *Das Reich* would be unable to help engage in the coming clash with 6th Guards Tank Army. Where was Breith's command?

III Panzer Corps

It was only on 9 July, after five days of costly fighting, that III Panzer was able to extricate itself from the dense Soviet minefields and defensive lines and begin its long-delayed advance to the north. By this time, it was many days behind schedule, the three panzer divisions should have been in the vicinity of Prokhorovka. A combined thrust from the north-east by 6th Panzer and 19th Panzer had finally led to the fall of the Belgorod heights and the destruction of two enemy divisions. It was thus only on the 10th that III Panzer Corps could begin its advance northward. This had been achieved at no little cost in tank numbers.

10 July was another frustrating day. Of III Panzer Corps' three panzer divisions only the 6th was available for the thrust northward as both 7th and 19th were still tied down trying to contain the growing number of assaults on Kempf's eastern flank. In this, Vatutin's strategy mirrored that he was employing on the western

flank against 48th Panzer Corps: attack the wings and thus deny the enemy the opportunity to fully engage his resources on his frontal assault. Thus on 6th Panzer's western flank, 19th Panzer was employed giving support to 168th Infantry Division as it cleared Soviet forces from the eastern bank of the northern Donets. 7th Panzer was facing a worse situation. It had been unable to free itself from the work of assisting the three infantry divisions of *Korps Raus* in their unenviable role as protectors of the eastern flank of Detachment Kempf. German losses in these formations were increasing significantly as the Soviets continually reinforced their units. It is therefore hardly surprising that 6th Panzer's forward momentum was slow, dogged by a succession of enemy defensive lines astride their line of march.

This did not prevent Manstein from exhorting Kempf to get his forces moving northward. With the beginning of the SS Panzer Corps' advance on Prokhorovoka, the Field Marshal stressed how important it was that Breith's command achieve a rapid breakthrough. He must ensure that all three panzer divisions be on hand to assist the Waffen SS to defeat the massed ranks of the 5th Guards Tank Army. Kempf was to do whatever was necessary to ensure that III Panzer Corps would be available in toto to begin the drive alongside the SS divisions on the 11th. Nor was Manstein oblivious to the implications of the news that on the northern face of the salient, Ninth Army was already staring defeat in the face.

On 10 July, the British and Americans had landed in Sicily.

SS Panzer Corps and 5th Guards Tank Army

Squalls of rain accompanied the resumption of the SS divisions' attack. Hoth had ordered the Luftwaffe to concentrate its efforts on supporting the attack towards Prokhorovka despite the weather. At 0500, the 2nd Panzer Regiment of the *Leibstandarte* in SPWs with armour support provided by medium panzers, four Tigers, StuGs and assorted *panzerjäger* advanced either side of the Prokhorovka road – which lay just over 7km away – and came under heavy artillery fire. The initial objective was the heavily fortified Hill 252.2, which had to be secured before the final thrust on the town could be made. As the formation made passage it came under tank attacks on either flank, the tanks emerging from the village of Andreevka to the north and the forest to the west of Jamki in the south. Although the hill was reached by 0625 it was discovered that the Soviets had dug a large and deep anti-tank trench from the hill, north to the *Oktabrisky* State Farm. As the obstacle could not be crossed they had to halt and await the arrival of bridging equipment.

Unbeknownst to the Germans, the first units of the massive reinforcement descending on the area from Steppe Front had arrived overnight as the mass of 5th Guards Tank Army was beginning to deploy in the fields around the town. Rotmistrov had set to work drawing up a deployment whereby his forces could execute the order he had received from Vatutin early on the 12th. He was to 'deliver a counterstroke in the direction of Komsomolets State farm and Pokrovka and, in co-operation with 5th Guards and 1st Tank Army, destroy the enemy in the Kotchetovka, Pokrovka and Greznoye regions and do not permit him to with draw in a southerly direction.'

As artillery and air strikes began to pound Hill 252, other forces from the *Leibstandarte* fanned out to provide flank cover for the 2nd Regiment. To the north the reconnaissance battalion supported by *panzerjäger* fought with numerous T-34s throughout the day whilst to the south, two battalions form the 1st Regiment crossed the railway line and found themselves engaged in heavy fighting for the remainder of the day and the night to come for Storozhevoe.

The *Leibstandarte* could not call upon *Das Reich* for assistance as its forces were being very effectively pinned down to the south. Attempts by *Das Reich* to advance and secure the village of Vinogradovka were thwarted by the continual assaults of skilfully handled armour of the 26th Tank Brigade and supporting infantry. It was only in the late morning that the first bridge across the Psel was completed allowing the first medium panzers to cross to assist the troops of *Totenkopf* that had fought throughout the night to defend the small bridgehead. By day's end, Hill 222.6 had still not been captured while on the south bank of the Psel the *Eicke* grenadier regiment supported by the divisional StuG unit captured the village of Vasileyvka but was unable to advance farther in the face of powerful Soviet resistance. These two formations had not been able to provide the flank protection for *Leibstandarte* that Hausser's plan had called for.

The bridging of the tank ditch shortly after midday was followed by the main assault by the panzer regiment on Hill 252.2, which was captured by 1300 hours. Thereafter, the Germans swung round to the north-west and attacked the heavily fortified state farm with its dug-in KV and T-34s and PaKs, and under heavy artillery fire from batteries in the Psel valley. It too was captured, but by now the division was dangerously exposed with open flanks and thus out of necessity in the late afternoon it was halted with its foremost units just 2 kilometres from the outskirts of Prokhorovka.

The orders issued by Hausser for the following day were quite specific about divisional responsibilities.

a) *Totenkopf* was to capture Hill 226.2 and thereafter it was to thrust along the north bank of the river Psel, cut the Orel-Prokhorovka road thereby providing cover to the left flank of the *Leibstandarte*.

b) *Das Reich* was to provide cover to the left flank of the *Leibstandarte* by the capture of Storozhevoe and Vinogradovka. It was then to thrust south of Prokhorovka.

c) The main offensive effort would be carried out by the *Leibstandarte*. However, the orders were clear that the advance was to be made in conjunction with *Totenkopf* once Hill 226 had been captured. LAH was to capture Prokhorovka and Hill 252.4

Thus by day's end the runes had been cast on the German side for their role in the events of the 12th.

On the 'other side of the hill' Rotmistrov was now having to contend with what seems to have been a totally unexpected advance by the Germans towards Prokhorovka that now rendered void Vatutin's orders for 5th Guards Tank Army to launch a counteroffensive the following day.

6–12 July Ninth Army

The first intimation the Germans had that Rodin's hastily re-deployed 2nd Tank Army was in the process of launching a major attack was shortly after 0200, when probing attacks were followed at 0350 by the main body of Soviet armour. T-34s and T-70s of the 107th and 164th Tank Brigades supported by infantry and heavy air cover attacked in waves and by 0600 a heavy tank battle was being fought between the villages of Ssoborowka and Samadorowka. By mid-morning the Russian assault had been contained and thrown back.

Model responded by releasing 2nd and 9th Panzer Divisions and these were heavily engaged by mid-morning. German tank numbers began to climb. 2nd Panzer was fielding over 100 panzers and was supported by 24 Tigers of 505 and a number of attached StuG brigades. With 20th Panzer on its left and 9th Panzer on its right the Germans were fielding a phalanx of 300 tanks on a frontage of barely 12 kilometres between Ssaborowka and Ponyri 1. Rodin now threw against them his 3rd Tank Corps to serve alongside his surviving armour from earlier in the morning. The resulting clash was to prefigure in spectacle on a slightly smaller scale the famous encounter at Prokhorovka a few days hence.

2nd Panzer Division had been tasked with effecting a breach in the enemy's second defence line and of capturing the hamlet of Kashara that lay in the lee of the Olkhavatka heights. Advancing in an armoured wedge across rolling wheat fields the division was screened by the Tigers of 505. The Tigers came to halt to engage

TIGER HUNT

'He [the Tiger] fired at me from literally one kilometre away. His first shot blew a hole in the side of my tank. With his second, he hit my axle. At a range of half a kilometre, I fired at him with a special calibre shell, but it bounced off him like a candle. I mean, it did not penetrate his armour … He started looking for me, turning his turret to see where I was'.

Ivan Sagun, T-34 commander. Sagun withdrew under cover and survived the encounter.

at maximum range the Soviet armour that was emerging from the copses and folds in the ground, with their guns firing fusillades up to 30 in number. They in their turn were screened by plunging artillery fire and long-range mortars. Model had ordered that the assets of Luftflotte 6 be allocated to serve this one primary thrust, as it was here, on his primary offensive axis, that he expected his breakthrough to be made. Discernible above the din were the distinctive howls of the German werfers and Soviet katyushas their smoke trails crossing the sky.

In the face of such pressure, the Russian forces were pushed back but at the same time were inflicting heavy casualties on the Germans. Rodin's anti-tank guns and artillery had been used to supplement those in the defences and on ground devoid of cover, even heavily armoured Tigers and Ferdinands began to be knocked out. Such was the ferocity of the fighting that lasted through to evening that just six Tigers were still operating at nightfall. Despite this massive effort by the Germans they had been unable to reach Kashara. One of the consequences of his losses to Tigers was that Rokossovsky had many of his T-34s dug in.

The savagery on this axis was matched by that in the contest for the village and railway station at Ponyri and on the approach to MaloArchangelsk. On the former, rolling forward in support of the infantry divisions in an arc that embraced the northern part of Ponyri I through to the railway, came 9th Panzer Division with its medium Mark IIIs and IVs alongside the surviving Ferdinands of PanzerJäger Regiment 656, with Funklenk B.IVs dealing with the minefields. Participants in this attack spoke of 'artillery in amounts we have never seen before' falling on them as they tried to advance. Those panzers, assault guns, Ferdinands and infantry that were able to thread their way through the breaches in the minefields caused by the demolition vehicles immediately found themselves embroiled in ferocious battles amidst the houses and buildings of Ponyri. Each had been fortified with machine guns, 45mm and 76mm anti-tank guns, mortars and flame throwers. The ferocity of the close combat fighting was likened to that of Stalingrad. No quarter was shown by either side. Ponyri was still in Soviet hands at nightfall.

To the east of the railway stop the 78th Sturm Division, the 292nd Infantry Division supported by the surviving Ferdinands of PanzerJäger Regiment 656 and the assault guns of the 177th and 244th StuG brigades led the assault on the fortifications covering Point 253.3, which protected the approach to the village of Prilyepi. Here, too, the fighting was savage with many StuGs being lost to the deep minefields. The Germans wished to break through here at all costs in order to permit their mobile units to swing to the south-west into the rear of the Soviet positions defending the heights. While Hill 253.5 was taken on the 6th, the repeated attempts by the Germans to push farther south dissolved in the face of the strength of the enemy defence.

Freissner's XXIII Corps was having no greater success. The same recipe of reinforcement and of packing the defensive field with more mines, feeding in more infantry, fielding more artillery and katyusha batteries, served to increase the losses the Germans were experiencing. Advance beyond the railway junction at Protassovo proved impossible in the face of a ferocious defence. Aiding all Soviet units was the rising tempo of sorties being carried out by the Red Air Force as more units were flown in to bolster the air effort. Now the Germans found every attempt at advance being contested by heavy IL-2 strikes supported by large numbers of supporting Soviet fighters strafing the troops. The Luftwaffe was not so often to be seen as it was being overstretched and lack of POL supplies began to reduce the sortie rate. By day two of the offensive, Model's eastern flank had been halted and would remain that way, as his western forces had been on day one.

Indeed, by day two of the German offensive Rokossovsky was convinced that such was the narrowness of the front of the German assault he could risk pulling in units from either side of the developing German salient to reinforce his defences before the Olkhovatka heights. Tank units, infantry formations and masses of artillery were now brought in overnight and on succeeding nights to bolster his defences. He was creating a massive anvil on which he would succeed in the following days in shattering the German offensive hammer. This was a battle of attrition par excellence and whilst he could reinforce and replace his losses, Model could not. The commander of Central Front was beginning to sense even at the end of day two that the impaling of Model's forces on his defences was happening just as he had hoped. The task now was to ensure that the German commander committed all his reserves. Once that had happened, he would change the rules of this game.

On the following day, Model committed yet another panzer division from his shrinking armoured reserve to his main assault on the Ponyri–Olkhovatka axis. By dawn, 18th Panzer was deployed alongside 9th Panzer to the north of Ponyri in readiness for a thrust southward on a narrow frontage through the Soviet defence lines screening the approaches to Olkhovatka. Farther to the west, the 2nd and 20th Panzer Divisions were directed to attack the Soviet positions between Samodurovka and Kashara and thrust through to the village of Teploye. There seems to have been no reflection on Model's part as to the cost of the first two days' operations. He was continuing to feed in more and more tanks to replace those that had been lost – again, as with the German experience in the south, the term must be interpreted. Losses, as in total 'write offs' were surprisingly few. The third day of the offensive was to see no change in this formula, which was succeeding wonderfully in bleeding white his forces in exactly the manner anticipated by the Soviets.

Figures for tank losses notwithstanding, those among the German infantry were rising steeply with over 10,000 men falling on the first two days. Shortages in supplies were also becoming apparent by the 7th. German columns were being successfully attacked by wide-ranging and systematic Soviet air strikes on road convoys and railways halts close to and many miles behind the front lines. The on-going assault by partisan groups on railway communications carried on all through the offensive. This combined with the prodigious ammunition expenditure by his armour and artillery saw Model phoning Rastenburg and demanding that Zeitzler despatch 100,000 rounds of tank ammunition forthwith.

It was only at midday that the Germans managed to finally prise open a gap in the Soviet lines in the three-kilometre front between Samadorovka and Kashara, through which crashed the collective weight and firepower of 2nd and 20th Panzer Divisions. At the point of this phalanx were the Tigers of 505 – a number having been repaired overnight with passage through the minefields being blasted by the demolition vehicles of the Funklenk kompanie. Just 4 miles hence lay Teploye but Rokossovksy had packed- the gently rolling terrain between with the full paraphernalia of his defensive repertoire. In consequence, by day's end and in spite of the small German offensive and detachment on additional Luftwaffe units brought up from the southern sector, the attack had broken down in the face of ever thickening defences and fanatical Soviet resistance.

Model had no more joy in his further attempts to take Ponyri. Even the additional firepower of 18th Panzer alongside 9th Panzer was not enough to carry the battle, with the railway halt and other parts of the settlement changing hands throughout the day. At every turn the tanks and StuGs were confronted by the same unholy trinity of artillery, PaK and mines. No matter how great the scale of air attacks, it seemed to the Germans that the weight of fire from Soviet artillery was growing in intensity: and it was as Rokossovsky packed more and more batteries in and around Ponyri. Absorbing no fewer than five separate German assaults on Ponyri during the course of the day Major-General Yenshin's 307th Rifle Division saw each wilt and recoil amidst a storm of steel. Such was also the fate of the forces attempting to take MaloArchangelsk, as every offensive effort broke down in the face of the overwhelming firepower of the Soviet heavy guns and yet more freshly laid minefields.

As dawn broke on the 8th, the German forces deployed just a few kilometres to the north of Teploye and Olkhovatka were reinforced by 4th Panzer Division. This formation enabled Model to concentrate five panzer divisions along a frontage of just ten miles. Running from west to east from the villages of Molotych-Samadorovka through to Ponyri were the 20th, 4th, 2nd, 9th and 18th Panzer Divisions

Soviet infantry await the order to move to the front. They have the characteristic uniform and weapons of the summer of 1943.

deployed shoulder to shoulder. Although the four committed earlier had suffered losses, the collective weight and firepower of over 300 Mark IIIs, IVs and assault guns plus 26 Tigers gave Model hope that he could at last achieve his aim.

The overture to what would become a savage day's fighting was the first of the massed barrages from Soviet artillery and rocket batteries. German veterans still speak in awe of the sheer scale of the enemy bombardment as the whole of the southern horizon was lit up by this false dawn. The sense that the Soviet fire was actually increasing in scale from that of the previous days was not wrong. Rokossovsky had spent the previous day and the hours of darkness taking yet more formations from the quieter sectors of his Front and using them to augment his defensive positions in front of and to the rear of Teploye and Olkhovatka. In total, he had bolstered his line with two rifle divisions, an artillery division, an armoured rifle brigade and two armoured brigades. To provide the latter he had had to draw on his last such asset, which had been deployed to cover the southern approaches to Kursk against a breakthrough by 4th Panzer Army.

Here was proof of the damage being visited upon the Russian tank formations as the bulk of Rokossovsky's armour lay shattered on the battlefield or fixed in hull-down positions. The Soviet commander described these two tank brigades as 'our last hope'. Yet, in spite of the losses being inflicted upon his forces by a concentration of German firepower never before experienced, Rokossovsky was more than satisfied that his defences were nonetheless fulfilling their purpose. Each attack launched by the Germans was requiring them to commit more and more of armour to replace the wreckage of knocked out machines that marked the limited advance.

The German assault was ferocious – heavy Luftwaffe strikes preceded the advance of fists of armour that drove towards the Soviet positions through a hail of 'crash booms', anti-tank rifles, *katyusha* fire and heavy artillery. The mines brought a number to a halt as tracks were shattered and crews attempted to bail out

A mined StuG. Although rarely destroyed by such weapons, the damage to a StuG's suspension could require some days to repair.

amid a storm of small arms fire. Throughout the morning the Soviets did their utmost to hold back this great phalanx but to no avail. By midday, the Germans had, at heavy loss, effected a breach in the enemy lines through which now poured more than 200 panzers, which thereafter resolved into two separate thrusts directed at Teploye and southward through to the heights, above which lay the prize of Olkhovataka.

It took repeated assaults by the Germans, in what became a see-saw encounter of great savagery, before Teploye fell to them late in the day. The ejected Soviets fell back on pre-prepared positions dug into the hillside of the village and on the ridgeline from where they continued to rain down a ferocious storm of fire. This line constituted the final barrier before the prized open steppe beyond. Over the next few days the Germans launched waves of extremely costly and increasingly desperate assaults up the hillside, supported by air strikes. Tank assaults wilted in the hurricane of Soviet artillery fire called down upon them and infantry losses rose dramatically.

A Panzer III used as a command vehicle for Borgward demolition vehicles.

Both at Olkhovatka and Ponyri the German experience mirrored that of the attackers at Teploye. Like the wash and backwash of waves on a beach, German assault was followed by Soviet counter-assault. Panzers and StuGs manoeuvred rapidly to provide cover for the *landsers* of 6th Inf Div as they attempted to push forward up the slopes. Hill 274, deemed to be the linchpin of Soviet defences covering the western approaches to Olkhovatka, became the scene of hellish fighting. At Ponyri, Hill 253.5 held out as a massive breakwater to the German tide east of the village. In the village itself, the endless vicious fighting resolved around possession of the water tower, railway station, school and tractor works.

The inability of the Germans to secure the desired breakthrough led Model to issue an order late on the 8th to his Corps commanders that their objective now must be to engage in 'a rolling battle of attrition'. Such a fundamental shift shows Model's acceptance that the storming of the Olkhovatka heights and securing a breakthrough to Kursk was simply beyond his resources. Strength returns indicated that 50,000 infantry had fallen and 400 tanks and StuGs had been lost or were out of action for an advance of just a few kilometres.

The only ray of hope for the Germans came on the 9th when Hill 239, lying to the east of Ponyri was finally stormed with the prospect of carrying the village and thereafter rolling up the Olkhovatka position by a thrust for the north-east. However, this could not be realised unless the massively fortified Hill 253.5 to the north of Prilepy and thus astride the German right flank had also been neutralised. With the region to the rear of the hill still in Soviet hands, the Red Army continued to supply the position and pack 253 with every weapon that could be jammed onto its slope. Even with the support of the remaining Ferdinands of the 654th Abteilung, all attempts to take the hill on the 10th were thwarted.

It was not just Model who sensed that his enterprise was failing. Stalin too had expressed the view to Zhukov that the time was surely ripe to launch the planned counteroffensive. Zhukov concurred, confidently observing, 'Here, on the sector of the Central Front, the enemy no longer has at its disposal forces capable of breaking through our defences.' Stalin gave the go-ahead for the launch of Operation *Kutuzov* on 11/12 July. This would serve to relieve the pressure on the Central Front and give Rokossovsky time to regroup his forces prior to launching his counteroffensive in the days thereafter. By then, due to the unfolding threat to its rear and the need to divert forces northward in an attempt to contain it, Ninth Army would be unable to consolidate on any of its hastily constructed defences within the salient. Zhukov had determined that despite the ferocity that would attend the continuing German attacks they would in reality be the last desperate attempts to salvage an offensive already beyond redemption.

It happened exactly as Zhukov forecast. It was into the line between Ponyri and Prilyepi that on the 10th Model launched the last of his reserves. But even the commitment of the 10th Panzer Grenadier Division with its fresh resources could not help carry

A Ferdinand captured by Soviet troops of the 129th Rifle Division in the village of Alexandrovka.

the day. Ponyri remained in Soviet hands. The exhaustion now attendant on all the German units drawn up across Ninth Army's frontage was plain to see and with all reserve formations now committed within the salient, Model had nothing more to offer to force the issue. The entry in the OKW war diary for the 11th commenting on the efforts of the previous day, had rung the changes in Ninth Army's tactics in a manner that echoed Model's own shift of a few days before, thereby tacitly signalling the failure of *Zitadelle* in the north of the salient.

Although Model has realised that the writing had been on the wall for Ninth Army's offensive some days earlier, events to the north of the salient on 11 July proved beyond doubt that the game was up. All through the day, Russian units had been conducting large-scale reconnaissance sorties in strength across the frontage of the tank-denuded 2nd Panzer Army, tasked with defending the Orel salient and protecting the rear of Model's forces. These probings were clearly the harbingers of an imminent offensive, to be directed, it was assumed, at the rear of Ninth Army with the intention of eliminating all German forces therein.

12–17 July: Prokhorovka

Between the Psel and the Orel–Prokhovka Railway

In the dying hours of the 11th, Rotmistrov had no choice but to redraw his plan for the following day. The unexpected advance of the *Leibstandarte* to within a few kilometres of Prokhorovka now found the Germans halted amid the very fields that he had earlier earmarked for his own tank formations as the jumping-off positions for the defunct counteroffensive. The priority now was to deny the enemy Prokhorovka at whatever cost, as the loss of the town would unravel the whole Soviet position in the south of the salient.

The task was completed by 0200 with his tank units marshalled into new jumping-off points. Although now deployed some kilometres farther to the east than intended, four of the five corps available to Rotmistrov were stationed along a line stretching from the Psel through to Belenikhino, 15 kilometres to the south.

Allocated the task of confronting the *Leibstandarte* were the 18th and 29th Tank Corps of 5th Guards Tank Army; the former with 190 tanks and SPGs deployed along a 2km line running from the river through to a point just east of the *Oktabrisky* collective farm; the latter, fielding 212 tanks, was allocated the sector southward through to Storozhevoe. South of this point, and facing *Das Reich* was 2nd Guards Tank Corps along with the depleted 2nd Tank Corps. These formations could field 187 tanks. In reserve, to the east of Prokhorovka, was the 5th Guards Mechanised Corps with a further 223 tanks and SPGs. Yet further reinforcement was allocated by Vatutin in the form of an SPG regiment and three artillery and two *katyusha* regiments. Rotmistrov's command thus had available tank and SPG numbers much greater than that of

GENERAL ROTMISTROV

'We had to prepare anew, select artillery firing positions, deployment and attack lines. In compressed time, we had to refine missions, organise co-operation between corps and units, revise the schedule for artillery support and do all to facilitate the precise command and control of forces.'

General Pavel Rotmistrov

Nikita Krushchev, front commissar, discusses the situation facing 5th Guards Tank Army with its commander, General Pavel Rotmistrov, on 11 July.

the SS Panzer Corps. In total, he could field 793 tanks – 501 being T-34s, 261 T-70s, 31 Churchill Mark IVs, 37 SPGs and the 53rd Guards Independent Tank Regiment, with 21 KV-1s.

Numbers alone do not tell the whole story. T-70s and Churchills were of dubious value and even the T-34s were accepted as being vulnerable. Indeed, Katukov had expressed the view that his 1st Tank Army had suffered considerably at the hands of the panzers, albeit attributing most of his losses to Tigers and Ferdinands. Rotmistrov assumed that the SS divisions, being elite units, would be fielding large numbers of both. They were in error. No Ferdinands operated in the south of the salient.

The Russians would have been genuinely surprised how few of the feared Tigers were serviceable on the morning of 12 July, with just 14 spread across the three divisions. *Totenkopf* was fielding ten, *Leibstandarte Adolf Hitler* four and *Das Reich* none. Although the four serving with the *Leibstandarte* would account for a good number of Soviet tanks in the coming battle, by far and away the majority would fall to the 75mm guns of Panzer IVs, StuGs and Panzerjägers and the 50mm rifles of the Mark IIIs. The Corps was fielding 294 tanks and SPGs on 12 July spread across the three divisions. The strongest was *Totenkopf* with 121 machines, *Das Reich* had 103 and the *Leibstandarte*, which was to bear the brunt of 5th Guards Tank Army's assault during the course of the day, was actually the weakest with 70 tanks and assault guns. German strength was also raised by numbers of *panzerjäger*.

During the course of the 12th, 1000 Soviet and German tanks – of the 5th Guards Tank Army and 1st Tank Army and the II SS Panzer Corps – would see action in a series of surging encounters lasting hours at a time in an arc running from *Totenkopf*'s bridgehead on the northern bank of the Psel southward through to the village of Belenikhino. What has since come to be known as 'the great tank battle of Prokhorovka' was more specifically just one facet of this confrontation, albeit the largest in the clash of *Leibstandarte* with the 18th and 29th Tank Corps between the river Psel and the Belgorod–Kursk railway – a narrow battlefield

Operation Zitadelle 1943

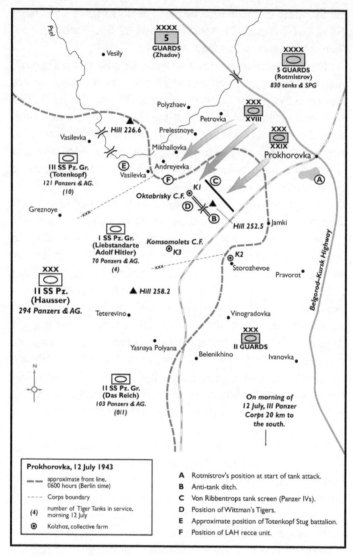

The tank battle of Prokhorovka on 12 July has achieved legendary status as the greatest clash of armour in history. Although a tactical German victory, the price paid by 5th Guards Tank Army contributed to the strategic victory of the Red Army in the Battle of Kursk.

selected by Hausser and Rotmistrov because it offered the best terrain for their tanks.

It was the prospect of encountering superior German tanks that now prompted Rotmistrov to bring forward the time of attack on the *Leibstandarte* by one and a half hours to 0630 (Berlin time). He hoped thereby to find the Germans in the process of preparing for theirs, and thus unready.

He placed 290 tanks in his first echelon, leaving fewer than 100 for his second wave. All drivers were instructed to close with the enemy at speed so as reach the critical distance of 500 metres when their 76mm guns would become effective. They would then 'swamp' the panzers, with the Tigers and Ferdinands – of which it is was assumed there would be many –as the priority targets. A mere four to five minutes would elapse from the moment the T-34s and T-70s gunned their engines and began their race towards the enemy positions until they were amongst them, with success and survival turning on catching the Germans unprepared.

South of Prokhorovka was a large orchard that covered the northern slopes of Hill 230.5, and it was here that Rotmistrov was ensconced to watch the battle unfold in the hours ahead. His hope of pre-empting the *Leibstandarte* evaporated before his eyes as at 0620 the panzers started to advance behind an explosive screen laid down by the divisional artillery and the Luftwaffe. To this was soon added that of the Soviets. As the panzers began fanning out by company to put space between one another in the face of the ferocious enemy bombardment, some kilometres to the east the Soviet first echelon gunned its engines and then with the code word for the attack: 'Stal! Stal! Stal! (Stalin) sounding across the radio net, nearly 300 T-34s and T-70s lurched forward. Rotmistrov observed that both sides went over to the offensive almost simultaneously.

The first intimation the Germans had of the avalanche of armour accelerating towards them was a cloud of dust on the horizon, followed shortly after by a wall of purple flares rising into the air warning of tank attack. The first panzers to react and open fire were the four Tigers under the command of Michael Wittman deployed near the *Oktybriski* farm. The superior optics in the Tigers and the long range of their 88mm main gun enabled them to start firing on the oncoming tanks of the 18th Tank Corps at 1800 metres. By the time the enemy had closed to 1000 metres, every shot was a direct hit. Rotmistrov's greatest fear – that his tanks would be caught in the open by an enemy able to exploit his superior range in gunnery – now came to pass as the first T-34s and T-70s were ripped apart by high velocity, armour-piercing ammunition.

It was unfortunate for the Soviet tankers that visibility was excellent. The panzers were therefore operating in near optimum conditions for a major tank engagement. As the Soviets continued to close to between 1000–800 metres, the 75mm guns of the Mark IVs and StuGs opened up. In such conditions, the highly trained and experienced German crews may have fired at four,

Only 14 Tigers fought at Prokhorovka on 12 July. Ten belonged to Totenkopf *and just four to the* Leibstandarte. Das Reich *had none serviceable on that day.*

T-34s race at speed towards the Germans in the battle at Prokhorovka.

even five rounds per minute. Tanks erupted as their frontal armour was penetrated and the ammunition within exploded, turrets flew skyward while the blazing hulks of shattered tanks collided with one another.

Then the surviving Soviet tanks were amidst the panzers and combat degenerated into a ferocious melee. With so many machines racing around one another, success came to the tank commander who reacted instantly to a target and to crews who reacted instantly to his voice commands. Soon the battlefield was littered with the shattered remains of gutted and blazing armour – the bulk of which was Russian – with thick black oily smoke drifting across the terrain, making accurate gunnery increasingly difficult for both sides.

Although the first assault had been driven off by 0900 hours, 15 minutes later another series of rolling attacks all across the front between the river and the embankment began, as Rotmistrov released his second echelon. Packs of T-34s sortied from Jamki and Prokhorovka under heavy artillery and air support. The subsequent engagement was conducted at high speed.

Between 1100 and 1130 the Soviets managed to breach the German line. Four T-34s managed to destroy two 150mm guns before being knocked out. There was a breakthrough near Hill 252 but this too was repulsed.

ROLLING WITH THE ENEMY

Four of the seven panzers used by 6th Panzer Regiment of the *Leibstandarte* were put out of commission at a distance of 220 metres. The remaining three joined the ranks of the advancing Russian tanks and moved with the pack into the range of the II Panzer Regiment of the *Leibstandarte* located about 800 metres to the rear. These three could fire at the Russians from a distance of 10 to 30 metres and make every shell a direct hit because the Russians could not see through the dust and smoke that there were German tanks rolling with them in the same direction. There were already nineteen Russian tanks standing burning on the battlefield when the Abteilung opened fire for the first time. The IInd/Abteilung destroyed about 62 T-70s and T-34s in a three-hour battle that could almost be termed hand-to-hand combat.

The German Offensive

Although the Germans had been shaken by the scale and ferocity of the Soviet assaults, sufficient of the *Leibstandarte*'s armour was operational for them to begin an attack on Prokorovka in the late afternoon. Such had been the losses in the two tank corps that Rotmistrov had to call up his sole reserve formation. The 120 tanks of the 5th Guards Mechanised Corps, 10th Guards Mechanised Brigade and 24th Guards Tank Brigade moved out. Once more, there began the *danse macabre*, but on this occasion the Russians got the better of the encounter. In failing light and deteriorating weather conditions, the German advance petered out.

Despite the day's exertions and the very heavy losses that the panzers of the *Leibstandarte* had inflicted on Rotmistrov's command, the combatants were to spend the night in virtually the same positions in which they had begun the day. 5th Guards Tank Army still held Prokhorovka and the Germans had once again been denied their prize. Counting their losses and recouping what strength they could, both sides girded themselves for a resumption of combat at first light.

The Northern and Southern Flanks

Given the importance attached by Hausser to *Totenkopf*'s early capture of Hill 226 and thereafter drive rapidly to the north-east to cover the flank of the advancing *Leibstandarte*, the fighting on this sector would prove to be every bit as severe. Indeed, it would cost *Totenkopf* half of its armoured strength by day's end.

The 60-ton bridge across the Psel had finally been completed at dawn and the ten Tigers crossed to join the medium panzers already there. By mid-morning, all the division's armour bar a detachment of StuGs was on the north bank. The assault on Hill 226 had gone in at midday and the resulting fighting was savage. Extensively fortified, it had been under continual attack by the Germans from the air, with artillery, werfers and armour. Even though reinforced by the first units of Zhadov's 5th Guards Army which was just arriving on the scene, it fell by 1300 hours. But immediate German attempts to push to the north-east were thwarted and fighting continued for the greater part of the afternoon. Following a rapid re-grouping, a further German attack in the early evening in the face of declining weather conditions and heavily supported by the Luftwaffe at last saw the division achieve a breakthrough. Led by the Tigers, the enemy defences were breached and as darkness fell the Death's Head troops had secured the village of Polyzhaev while the heavy panzers pushed forward to the Beregovoy/Kartshevka road. Although the Germans would not know it at the time, this would mark the most northerly point they would secure in the south of the salient.

To the south of the railway line, *Das Reich* had also been involved in heavy fighting, albeit not involving such masses of armour. Only the *Deutschland* regiment had been allocated an offensive role and it found the going extremely difficult, in consequence of which the 2nd SS Division was unable to give any significant assistance to the *Leibstandarte* during the course of the day. Throughout the morning it weathered heavy Soviet tank assaults in its attempt to take Storozhevoe. As usual, the village had been heavily fortified and each building had to be taken in hand-to-hand combat with only the southern part taken by mid-afternoon.

By midday, *Das Reich* forces were being assailed from the south and south-east by the combined armour of 2nd Tank Corps and 2nd Guards Tank Corps forcing the SS troops on to the defensive across the whole of their frontage. This assault only slackened when one of the remaining tank brigades had to be sent south to strengthen the forces containing the III Panzer Corps as it strained to break out of its bridgehead on the northern Donets. By evening, the tempo of the fighting had dropped off as mutual exhaustion and the worsening weather brought fighting to a halt.

Despite the unprecedented scale of the fighting, and the massive tank losses the Germans had inflicted on 5th Guards Tank Army – with some 400 T-34s and T-70s out of action by 13 July – II SS Panzer Corps had realised none of the objectives set for it by Hausser in his orders of the evening of the 11th. It is for this

5th Guards Tank Army lost nearly 400 tanks at Prokhorovka but that was the price that had to be paid to stop the SS Panzer Corps. Here an SS officer examines T-34s knocked out by German panzers.

reason that the Russians argue that Prokhorovka was a Soviet, not a German victory.

The Conference at Rastenburg

Both von Kluge and von Manstein received a summons late on the 12th to attend a conference with Hitler on the following day at his East Prussian HQ. Once there, it did not take long for him to reveal his concerns. Following the allied invasion of Sicily and the poor resistance put up by the Italian forces, he was concerned that other landings would soon follow elsewhere on the Italian mainland or the Balkans. The only forces he could draw on to send to Italy would have to come from the Kursk front. He was therefore forced to cancel *Zitadelle*. It is also likely that he already concluded that the Eastern offensive had failed.

The commander of Army Group Centre was only too happy to accept official confirmation of what was already a de facto reality for Ninth Army, with its assault having been stalled since the 10th. Furthermore, he was now looking at a potentially dire situation as the Soviets had just launched a massive counteroffensive against the Orel salient, in the rear of Ninth Army. To address this he had already sanctioned Model's transfer of 12th Panzer and 36th Motorised Infantry Division northward to support 2nd Panzer Army. 18th and 20th Panzer Divisions were also ordered out of the Kursk salient later on the 13th. The outflow of these ostensibly offensive assets clearly ruled out any continuation of the offensive within it. Indeed, Kluge asserted categorically that 'there could be no possibility of continuing *Zitadelle*' or of resuming the operation at a later date.

Manstein however, argued strongly against an immediate cessation, wishing to destroy 5th Guards Tank Army completely. Hitler's response was to allow him to the 17th to see out the job. Thereafter, all offensive operations in the south would be terminated and the SS Panzer Corps would be transferred to Italy. However, the Führer ordered the bulk of the remaining Luftwaffe assets in the south transferred to help operations in the Orel salient.

13–17 July

Although operations continued around Prokhorovka as Manstein desired, according to General Freidrich Fangohr, C of S of 4th Panzer Army, 'Faced with such superior Red Army forces *Obergruppenführer* Hausser could no longer think of continuing the attack on 12 or 13 July.'

Though III Panzer Corps finally managed to link up with 167th Infantry Division and *Das Reich* on the 15th thereby creating a more coherent German front to the west and south of Prokhorovka, the continuing clashes between the SS Panzer Corps and Rotmistrov's forces were inconclusive, albeit bloody and fierce. Russian resistance had been strengthened with the arrival of Marshal

Zhukov, who had been ordered to oversee operations around Prokhorovka by Stalin late on the 12th. On the 16th there was a growing sense of satisfaction pervading Zhukov's headquarters in Prokhorovka as reports flowing in throughout the day all spoke of a significant fall-off in enemy attacks across the Voronezh Front. For the Deputy Supreme commander it signalled that the German offensive in the south was finally spent. While the next few days were to be characterised by bloody stalemate, the Soviets recorded few, if any, probes by German armour.

So it was to remain until the German forces began a fighting retreat to their start lines a few days later, with the whole operation concluded by the 23 July. Operation *Zitadelle* had failed. For the Red Army, this ended the first phase of their defensive-offensive strategy.

THE LEGACY

Although Goebbels and his Propaganda Ministry moved very quickly to mask the failure of *Zitadelle* at home and broad, such dissembling could not conceal the truth amongst the ranks of the *Ostheer* or at Rastenburg. *Zitadelle* had realised none of the objectives set for it.

Zitadelle's immediate legacy had been to so weaken the re-equipped panzer and infantry formations that they were unable to fully assist Army Groups Centre and South counter the rash of massive counteroffensives that began on 12 July with the launch of Operation *Kutuzov*. In consequence, although German forces in the Orel salient and southward from Kharkov thence down to the Sea of Azov would continue to fight hard and inflict heavy casualties on the Soviets during the course of their post-*Zitadelle* operations, the great westward retreat the Germans began in mid-September – with its corresponding abandonment of almost all territory to the east of the river Dnieper – stemmed directly from the failure of *Zitadelle*. This was the case even though German losses in the battle, in both armour and infantry, were much lower than has often been assumed.

The legacy for the longer term was profound. The military initiative on the Eastern Front passed irrevocably to the Red Army. Guderian,

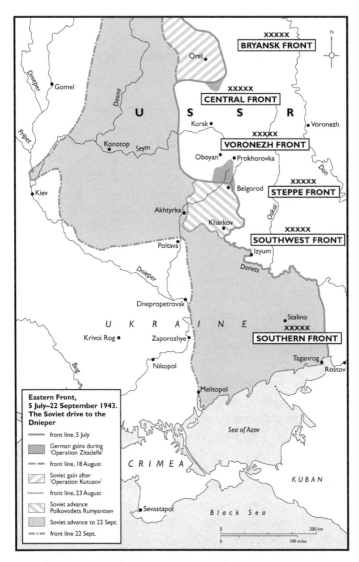

The consequences of defeat at Kursk for Germany are plain to see in this map. For the Red Army, the territorial gains and forced retreat of the Wehrmacht from the eastern Ukraine were the fruits of the defensive/offensive strategy embraced on 12 April 1943.

who as Inspector of Panzer Troops had overseen the partial rehabilitation of the tank arm and who had voiced his opposition to the operation from the outset, summed up the consequences for Germany of the defeat at Kursk:

> With the failure of *Zitadelle* we had suffered a decisive defeat. The armoured formations, reformed and re-equipped with so much effort, had lost heavily in both men and equipment [author's note – this was the perception at the time] and would now be unemployable for a long time to come. It was problematical whether they could be rehabilitated in time to defend the Eastern Front … Needless to say, the Russians exploited their victory to the full. There were to be no more periods of quiet on the Eastern Front. From now on, the enemy was in undisputed possession of the initiative.

Germany no longer possessed the resources that would permit it to reverse the military balance of power in the East. The capture of Berlin in May 1945 and the total defeat of Nazi Germany would follow the defeat of *Zitadelle*. We must, however be wary of identifying cause and effect with overconfidence. A qualification has to be added.

Even had the Germans achieved victory at Kursk (in the author's view, never a realistic prospect) it would have made no difference to the outcome of the war. Even before *Zitadelle* the strategic pendulum had swung decisively against Germany in every theatre of war in which the Reich was engaged. Although the war in the East was by far the greatest theatre in which the Wehrmacht was engaged, the conflict on this front was so huge that no one battle could settle its outcome. Indeed, the eminent German military historian Karl-Heinz Frieser, when writing of the German expectations of the battle, noted that Hitler, OKW and OKH appreciated that 'It was no longer possible to achieve a decisive victory on the eastern front, certainly not in a single battle.'

It was a confident Stalin who met Roosevelt and Churchill in Tehran some months after Kursk as he now knew that the outcome of the war in the East was no longer in doubt. He said as much publicly when speaking on the occasion of the twentieth anniversary of the October Revolution later in 1943.

If the Battle of Stalingrad signalled the twilight of the German Army, then the Battle of Kursk confronted it with catastrophe.

The Cost

What was the cost to the respective combatants of this great trial of strength? Let us first address the most contentious and singular issue which this battle seems forever associated – tank losses. Although it is not possible to present such with an absolute degree of certitude, it is nonetheless now possible to do so with greater confidence. What the figures do is repudiate the long-held view that Kursk was 'the death ride of the panzers'.

Of the total of 371 panzers and assault guns and Sturmpanzer IVs recorded as having been 'lost' – where the term equates to a total write-off – by Army Group Centre during July, just 88 of these occurred during the offensive phase of Ninth Army's operations, between 5–14 July. It thus follows that the greater number of 'write-offs' were suffered in the defensive operations suffered by the whole Army Group post-Kursk. These were incurred during the course of the massive defensive operations conducted by the armoured and motorised infantry of Ninth Army and 2nd Panzer Army as they fought to contain the Red Army's counteroffensive against the Orel salient, which had begun on 12 July and continued at a ferocious tempo into August.

Unsurprisingly, the total number of 'write-offs' in 4th Panzer Army and III Panzer Corps was higher with 190 panzers and assault guns having been destroyed between 5–17 July. This number was still remarkably low given the ferocity of the combat experienced. As in the case of Ninth Army, these numbers indicate a far lower number of total write-offs than was earlier assumed.

The figure of 278 machines written off destroys the 'death ride' myth. This is especially so given that these losses were substantially

WRITE-OFFS

4th Panzer Army and III Panzer Corps Panzer Losses
40 Panzer III, 79 Panzer IV, 44 Panther, 6 Tiger I, 18 StuGs, 3
Flammpanzer III
SS Panzer Corps Losses
5 Panzer III, 23 Panzer IV, 3 Tiger I, 5 StuGs

less that the total of 511 panzers and 306 assault guns that left the production lines in Germany during July.

The differential between the large number of AFVs 'knocked out' on a daily basis in Ninth Army, 4th Panzer Army and Armee Abteilung Kempf and the 278 machines written off in total by 17 July can be accounted for by the fact that in the offensive phase many of those rendered non-operational because of battle damage were recovered from the battlefield and sent back to the repair shops. A large number of those same machines, having suffered only short-term damage, were returned to combat within just a few days. It also follows that, given the large number of panzers and StuGs cycled through the recovery and repair procedure, more than a few hundred of them were attended to on more than one occasion during the course of the offensive. The highest number of machines under such repair for 4th Panzer Army was on 10 July, with 462 being worked on at day's end.

Not surprisingly, in view of the technical limitations under which Soviet armour laboured during the battle, tank losses in the Red Army were far higher. How high is dependent on the source. One Russian source dating to 1993, gives a figure for north and south of the salient of 1614 tanks and SPGs written off from a total of 5035 committed to the defensive operation, with the bulk being lost in the south. Other Soviet/Russian sources offer different figures. Drawing on figures compiled by the deputy commander of the tank and mechanised forces for the Red Army on 23 July 1943, Zetterling and Frankson, in a statistical study of the battle, calculate that of the total of 2924 tanks and SPGs committed to the Voronezh and Steppe Fronts between 4–20 July, 1254 were written off. This number is significantly greater than the 1993 Russian source for the Central, Voronezh and Steppe Fronts. Other more detailed figures offered by them include 313 write-offs by 15 July of the 634 tanks possessed by 1st Tank Army on 5 July. Those for 5th Guards Army suggest that 334 were totally destroyed in the four days 12–16 July. Percentage losses are 51 and 40 per cent of their initial strengths respectively (it is worth noting that one year later, the British Army would lose 314 tanks knocked out in two days, of which 140 were written off in Operation *Goodwood* in Normandy, facing essentially the same panoply of weaponry as deployed by the German Army at Kursk).

For the Red Army seeing down the German offensive in the salient was only the first stage of their defensive-offensive strategy, which also embraced Operations *Kutuzov* and *Polkovodets Rumyanstev*. For them, this is what constitutes their 'Kursk operation' and embraced the period from 5 July through to 23 August. Overall write-offs for that period are listed by the 1993 Russian source as 6064 tanks and SPGs. This averaged out to 121 tanks and SPGs written-off daily for that period. These are extremely high figures and serve to confirm once again the capacity of a reducing panzer force to still inflict disproportionate casualties on the enemy's tank arm (together with PaKs, artillery and aircraft).

The figure for manpower losses for the German Army during *Zitadelle* that has always had the greatest circulation is 70,000. This figure derived from Russian sources and implied that this number was for those killed. However, the Soviet General Staff Study on the battle quotes the same figure but has the qualifier 'dead and wounded'. As a maxim, the ratio of dead to wounded in German offensive operations throughout the conflict was 1:4. Zetterling and Frankson have concluded, after consulting Wehrmacht documentation, that casualties for the offensive period 5–11 July in the north and 4–20 July in the south amounted to 56,827. The number of dead in Ninth Army they quote as 3880, with total casualties, including wounded and missing, as 22,273; the difference

Despair and exhaustion on the faces of the German soldiers after having lost one of the greatest battles of the Second World War.

between this figure and 56,827 is made up by losses in the south of the salient through to 20 July. By way of comparison, total German losses in dead and wounded were therefore less than incurred by the British Army on the First Day of the Somme where there were 57,740 casualties, of which just under 20,000 were fatalities.

The Legacy

As with their armour, Soviet manpower losses were much higher on both faces of the salient with those incurred in the south far higher. The 1993 source states that losses in the south totalled 54,994 dead, wounded and missing. This is not dissimilar to the figures given by Manstein in his memoirs, where he lists 17,000 killed and 34,000 prisoners. The Russian source has total Soviet manpower losses for the whole of the defensive phase of the Kursk operation for all three fronts between 5–23 July as 177,847, with 70,330 of this number being dead and wounded.

Although this book has not attempted to deal with the air battle over the salient, it too was fought at a ferocious tempo. The reader is directed to the bibliography for books that deal with this aspect. However, Christer Bergstrom in his study *Kursk: The Air Battle* concludes that air losses in the north of the salient for the period 5–11 July amounted to 430 Soviet to 57 German and in the south, 677 Soviet to 220 German losses.

ORDERS OF BATTLE

German Army

Army Group South

Field Marshal Erich von Manstein

4th Panzer Army
Colonel-General Hermann Hoth

XLVIII (48th) Panzer Corps — General of Panzer Troops von Knobelsdorff

3rd Panzer Division — Lieutenant-General Westhoven

11th Panzer Division — Major-General Mickl (acting commander)

Panzer Grenadier Division *Grossdeutschland* — Lieutenant-General Hoernlein

167th Infantry Division — Lieutenant-General Trierenberg

II SS Panzer Corps — SS-Obergruppenführer Hausser

1 SS Panzer Grenadier Division *Leibstandarte Adolf Hitler* — SS-Brigadeführer Wisch

2 SS Panzer Grenadier Division *Das Reich* — SS-Gruppenführer Krüger

3 SS Panzer Grenadier Division *Totenkopf* — SS-Brigadeführer Priess

Orders of Battle

LII Army Corps
57th Infantry Division
255th Infantry Division
332nd Infantry Division

General of Infantry Ott
Major-General Fretter Pico
Lieutenant-General Poppe
Lieutenant-General Schaeffer

Army Detachment Kempf
General of Panzer Troops Kempf

III Panzer Corps
6th Panzer Division
7th Panzer Division
19th Panzer Division
168th Infantry Division

General of Panzer Troops Breith
Major-General von Hünersdorff
Major-General Freiherr von Funck
Lieutenant-General G. Schmidt
Major-General Châles de Beaulieu

XI Army Corps
106th Infantry Division
320th Infantry Division

General of Panzer Troops Raus
Lieutenant-General Forst
Major-General Postel

XLII Army Corps
39th Infantry Division
161st Infantry Division
282nd Infantry Division

General of Infantry Mattenklott
Lieutenant-General Loeweneck
Lieutenant-General Recke
Major-General Kohler

Army Group Centre

Field Marshal Gunther von Kluge

Ninth Army
Colonel Walter Model

XX Army Corps

45th Infantry Division

72nd Infantry Division
137th Infantry Division
251st Infantry Division

General of Infantry Freiherr von
Roman
Major-General Freiherr von
Falkenstein
Lieutenant-General Müller-Gebhard
Lieutenant-General Kamecke
Major-General Feltzmann

XLVI Panzer Corps
7th Infantry Division
31st Infantry Division
102nd Infantry Division
258th Infantry Division

General of Infantry Zorn
Lieutenant-General von Rappard
Lieutenant-General Hossbach
Major-General Hitzfeld
Lieutenant-General Höcker

XLVII Panzer Corps   General of Panzer Troops Lemelsen
2nd Panzer Division   Lieutenant-General Lübbe
6th Panzer Division   Lieutenant-General Grossman
9th Panzer Division   Lieutenant-General Scheller
20th Panzer Division   Major-General von Kessel

XLI Panzer Corps   General of Panzer Troops Harpe
18th Panzer Division   Major-General von Schlieben
86th Infantry Division   Lieutenant-General Weidling
292nd Infantry Division   Lieutenant-General von Kluge

XXIII Army Corps   General of Infantry Freissner
78th Sturm Division   Lieutenant-General Traut
216th Infantry Division   Major-General Schack
383rd Infantry Division   Major-General Hoffmeister

Soviet Army

Central Front

Army General K.K. Rokossovsky

13th Army   Lieutenant-General N.P. Pukhov
4th Army   Lieutenant-General P.L. Romanenko
65th Army   Lieutenant-General P.I. Batov
70th Army   Lieutenant-General I.V. Galanin.
2nd Tank Army   Lieutenant-General A.G. Rodin
16th Air Army   Lieutenant-General S.I. Rundenko

Voronezh Front

Army General N.F. Vatutin

6th Guards Army   Lieutenant-General I.M. Chistyakov
7th Guards Army   Lieutenant-General M.S. Shumilov
38th Army   Lieutenant-General N.E. Chibisov
40th Army   Lieutenant-General K.S. Moskalenko
69th Army   Lieutenant-General V.D. Kruchenkin
1st Tank Army   Lieutenant-General M.E. Katukov
2nd Air Army   Lieutenant-General S.A. Krasovsky

Steppe Military District became Steppe Front on 9 July (Stavka Reserve)

Colonel-General I.S. Konev

4th Guards Army	Lieutenant-General G.I. Kulik.
5th Guards Army	Lieutenant-General A.S. Zhadov
27th Army	Lieutenant-General S.G. Trofimenko
47th Army	Major-General P.M. Kozlov
53rd Army	Lieutenant-General I.M. Manarov
5th Guards Tank Army	Lieutenant-General P.A. Rotmistrov
5th Air Army	Lieutenant-General S.K. Goriunov

The principal Soviet tank serving in the armoured and mechanised formations of the Red Army at Kursk: the T-34.

The Hummel (Bumble Bee) self-propelled gun served in the heavy battery of the armoured-artillery detachment of 20th Panzer Division.

VISITING THE BATTLEFIELD

Although the Cold War has been over for quite some years it is still the case that you need a visa to visit Russia. That being said, it is now much easier to visit the battlefield of Kursk as the area corresponding to the salient lies fully within Russia with its southern border with the Ukraine beginning some 25 miles to the north of Kharkov (Kharkiv). Although it is possible for the individual traveller to make the journey, it is probably more convenient – assuming cost is not a paramount concern – to contact those companies now offering battlefield tours. There are quite a few and the Kursk battlefield is either taken in with a visit to Moscow and Volgograd (formerly Stalingrad) or can be added on to the itinerary for an extra charge. Because of the sheer size of the salient it is not surprising that such tours focus on a visit to Prokhorovka. It is here that the former Soviet Union and now the Russian state have built monuments to commemorate the battle and the fallen.

For those unable to visit the site(s) there are many internet sources dealing with the battle. Some sense of the size of the battlefield can be gleaned by examining Google Earth, which has good photo coverage of the area corresponding to the salient. Many of the smaller hamlets and villages noted in the text and on maps in this book have disappeared or been renamed.

FURTHER READING

Armstrong, Richard N., *Red Army Tank Commanders*, Schiffer Military History, 1994

Barnet, Corelli (Ed.), *Hitler's Generals*, Wiedenfeld and Nicholson, 1989

Bellamy, C., *Absolute War*, MacMillan, 2007

Glantz, D., *Colossus Reborn*, University Press of Kansas, 2005

_____ *Soviet Intelligence in War*, Routledge, 1990

Glantz, D. and House, J., *The Battle of Kursk*, University Press of Kansas, 1999

Glantz, D. and House, J., *When Titans Clashed*, University Press of Kansas, 1995

Haupt, W., *Army Group Centre*, Schiffer, 1997

_____ *Army Group South*, Schiffer, 1998

Healy, M., *Zitadelle – the German offensive against the Kursk salient 4 -17 July, 1943*, Spellmount 2008

Jentz, T., *Panzer Truppen* Vol.2, Schiffer, 1996

Krivosheev, G.F., *Soviet Casualties in the Twentieth Century*, Greenhill, 1997

Manstein, Erich von, *Lost Victories*, Greenhill, 1987

Maggenheimer, H., *Hitler's War*, AAP , 1998

Mellenthin, F.W., *Panzer Battles*, The History Press, 2008

Merridale, C., *Ivan's War*, Faber and Faber, 2005

Newton, S., *Hitler's Commander*, Da Capo, 2006

_____ *Kursk – The German View*, Da Capo, 2002

Overy, R., *Russia's War*, Allen Lane, 1997

Shtemenko, S.M., *The Soviet General Staff at War*, Progress Pub Co, 1985

Soviet General Staff Study; *The Battle of Kursk* (trans and ed by D.Glantz and H.S. Orenstein), Routledge, 1999

Tooze, Adam., *The Wages of Destruction*, Allen Lane, 2006

Volkogonov, D., *Stalin*, Weidenfeld and Nicholson, 1991

Warlimont, W., *Inside Hitler's Headquarters*, Presidio, 1964

Werth, A., *Russia at War*, Barrie and Rockliff, 1964

Ziemke, E.F., *Stalingrad to Berlin*, US Army Center of Military History, 1968

Zetterling, N. and Frankson, A., *Kursk 1943: A Statistical Analysis*, Routledge, 2000

INDEX

Army Detachment Kempf 16, 30, 34, 65, 83, 147

Army Group A 30

Army Group Centre 14, 33, 35, 57, 136, 141, 147, 153

Army Group South 11, 12, 20, 28, 32, 56, 57, 146, 153

Assault Gun/StuG III/Ferdinand 15, 44, 47, 48, 49, 55, 60, 69, 70, 77, 78, 83, 88, 89, 94, 106, 107, 116, 120, 127, 141, 142

Artillery German/Soviet 17, 41, 43, 48, 50, 51, 52, 61, 62, 66, 67, 70, 71, 73, 75, 76, 80, 81, 83, 85, 88, 89, 94, 99, 100, 104, 105, 108, 109, 112, 113, 115, 116, 117, 118, 119, 120, 121, 126, 127, 129, 132, 133, 143, 150

Borgward B.IV 70, 88

Breith, General Hermann 106, 110, 111, 147

Chistyakov, General I.M. 98, 79, 99, 149

Churchill, Winston 140

Churchill tank 127

Das Reich, SS Panzer Grenadier Division 18, 80, 82, 96, 97, 101, 103, 106, 109, 110, 112, 113, 125, 127, 130, 134, 136, 147

Donets, river 9, 13, 16, 22, 30, 57, 63, 83, 84, 86, 111, 134

Enigma 27

Focke-Wulf Fw-190 80

Ferdinand tank destroyer 15, 44, 48, 49, 60, 64, 70, 71, 72, 87, 88, 89, 91, 104, 115, 116

Grossdeutschland, Panzer Grenadier Division 17, 29, 44, 46, 48, 73, 76, 95, 96, 99, 100, 101, 103, 104, 105, 106, 107, 108, 146

Guderian, General Heinz 22, 23, 60, 72, 138

Hausser, Obergruppenfuhrer Paul 11, 12, 58, 101, 106, 109, 113, 129, 133, 134, 136, 146

Henschel Hs-129 80

Hitler, Adolf 7, 8, 9, 10, 11, 12, 13, 15, 18,
    20, 21, 22, 23, 32, 33, 34, 35, 36, 43,
    47, 48, 49, 52, 58, 58, 60, 69, 71, 72,
    73, 82, 97, 108, 127, 135, 136, 140,
    146, 153, 154
Hoth, General Hermann 12, 16, 33, 57,
    65, 76, 86, 99, 101, 105, 107, 109,
    111, 146

Katukov, General M.E. 81, 99, 105, 127,
    149
Kharkov 9, 11, 12, 13, 14, 32, 39, 73, 75,
    86, 138, 152
von Kluge, Field Marshal Gunter 18, 35,
    135, 147, 148
von Knobelsdorff, General 107, 146
Konev, General Ivan 39, 68, 99, 149
KV-1, KV-1S 52, 54, 55, 64, 67, 127

Leibstandarte Adolf Hitler, SS Panzer
    Grenadier Division 13, 18, 80, 82, 97,
    108, 127, 146
'Lucy', spy ring 27, 71, 72

Manstein, Field Marshal Erich von 9, 10,
    11, 12, 14, 18, 20, 22, 23, 32, 35, 38,
    52, 60, 67, 69, 71, 109, 111, 135, 136,
    145, 146, 153
Model, Colonel General Walter 15, 16,
    17, 29, 36, 41, 58, 68, 69, 86, 87, 89,
    91, 93, 114, 115, 117, 118, 119, 120,
    122, 123, 124

Oboyan 57, 63, 66, 99, 101, 103, 107,
    108
Operational Order No.5 14
Operational Order No.6 15, 23
Operation Barbarossa 7, 33, 35, 36, 37,
    41, 44, 72
Operation Kutuzov 17, 27, 28, 123, 138,
    143

Panther tank 44, 47, 54, 55, 60, 76, 78, 93,
    94, 100, 101, 142
Panzer III 43, 44, 48, 78, 122, 142
Panzer IV 44, 45, 48, 49, 54, 84, 127,
    141, 142
Prokhorovka 5, 16, 18, 57, 58, 99, 106,
    108, 109, 110, 111, 114, 125, 127,
    128, 129, 130, 131, 132, 133, 135,
    136, 137, 152
Psel, river 6, 17, 18, 29, 57, 58, 63, 83, 94,
    97, 98, 102, 103, 104, 107, 108, 109,
    112, 113, 125, 127, 129, 133

Rastenburg 5, 9, 20, 21, 72, 118, 135, 138
Rokossovsky, General Konstantin 15, 16,
    17, 37, 66, 71, 91, 93, 115, 117, 119,
    120, 123, 148
Rotmistrov, General Pavel 99, 112, 114,
    125, 126, 127, 129, 130, 132, 133,
    136, 149
Rzhev salient 14, 36

SS Panzer Corps 11, 12, 13, 18, 21, 29,
    44, 46, 57, 58, 76, 79, m80, 83, 86,
    94, 95
Stalin, Iosif 11, 14, 16, 17, 23, 24, 26, 27,
    38, 39, 42, 53, 61, 84, 98, 99, 103, 123,
    129, 137, 140, 141
Stalingrad 8, 9, 14, 32, 38
Stuka 76, 78, 86, 101, 106, 107, 109

Tiger tank 15, 44, 46, 47, 54, 55, 60, 70,
    78, 80, 82, 83, 85, 87, 89, 91, 94, 96,
    101, 104, 110, 111, 114, 115, 118,
    120, 127, 129, 130, 133, 134, 142
T-34 44, 47, 52, 53, 64, 67, 81, 82, 91, 94,
    96, 97, 99, 100, 103, 104, 105, 108,
    112, 113, 114, 115, 127, 129, 130,
    131, 132, 134, 135, 150
T-70 52, 54, 67, 81, 94, 114, 127, 129,
    130, 132, 134

Index

Totenkopf, SS Panzer Grenadier Division 18, 81, 83, 107, 106, 108, 109, 113, 127, 130, 133, 147

Vatutin, General Nikolai F 11, 38, 63, 66, 71, 94, 98, 99, 101, 102, 103, 108, 109, 111, 112, 114, 125, 149

Waffen SS see SS Panzer Corps
Wittman, Michael 130

Yakovlevo 83

Zeitzler, General Kurt 59, 60, 118
Zhadov, General 108, 133, 149
Zhukov, Marshal Georgi 14, 17, 23, 24, 25, 26, 27, 36, 37, 39, 71, 82, 99, 123, 137